MORAL DESERT

A Critique

Howard Simmons

University Press of America,® Inc.
Lanham · Boulder · New York · Toronto · Plymouth, UK

Copyright © 2010 by
University Press of America,® Inc.
4501 Forbes Boulevard
Suite 200
Lanham, Maryland 20706
UPA Acquisitions Department (301) 459-3366

Estover Road
Plymouth PL6 7PY
United Kingdom

All rights reserved
Printed in the United States of America
British Library Cataloging in Publication Information Available

Library of Congress Control Number: 2009943078
ISBN: 978-0-7618-5069-4 (paperback : alk. paper)

∞™ The paper used in this publication meets the minimum
requirements of American National Standard for Information
Sciences—Permanence of Paper for Printed Library Materials,
ANSI Z39.48-1992

CONTENTS

Preface	v
1. Quandaries of Desert	1
1.1 Gary Hart and the Selby Rail Disaster	1
1.2 Internalism versus externalism	4
1.3 Further development of internalism	6
1.4 Further problems with desert	8
1.5 Positive desert	13
Notes	15
2. The Implications of Determinism	19
2.1 Determinism, 'hard' and 'soft'	19
2.2 Frankfurt cases	22
2.3 Libertarianism	24
2.4 Determinism and morality	26
Notes	30
3. Retributivism	33
3.1 Introduction	33
3.2 Retributivism: a first look	34
3.3 Peter French and vengeance theory	39
3.4 Corlett's account: exposition	45
3.5 Corlett's account: critique	50
3.6 Negative retributivism and some thought experiments	58
Notes	60

4. A Utilitarian Approach to Punishment — 65
    4.1 Utilitarianism in general — 65
    4.2 The basic utilitarian arguments — 67
    4.3 Objections to utilitarian punishment and responses — 75
    4.4 A return to desert? — 80
    Notes — 83

5. Utilitarian Punishment in Detail — 87
    5.1 Guiding principles — 87
    5.2 The S-score algorithm — 92
    5.3 From S-scores to actual sentences — 99
    5.4 Case studies for the application of the algorithm — 101
    5.5 Exculpation — 105
    5.6 State punishment: concluding remarks — 113
    5.7 Punishment within the family — 114
    Notes — 117

6. Effort and Distributive Justice — 121
    6.1 Introduction — 121
    6.2 Sher versus Rawls — 122
    6.3 Distributive justice — 125
    Notes — 128

7. Morality and Blame — 131
    7.1 Hostility to wrongdoers — 131
    7.2 Sher on blame — 135
    Notes — 139

8. Conclusion: Desert Skeptics in a vengeful world — 141
    Notes — 142

Appendix — 143

References — 149

Index — 153

PREFACE

Although reason is the engine of philosophy, faith may be its inspiration. This book is written in the faith that people can be brought to see that penal policy should not be about public vengeance, but about effective, yet reasonably humane, crime control. Of course, it is unlikely that intellectual argument can achieve this alone, or even that it can be the primary influence. But my hope is that those who have to fight this battle at a practical level will find something here to provide rational support for their stance. Of course, the book has more purely intellectual aims as well, but I regard its 'real world' relevance as the most important.

I owe a great debt to Tom Sorell. He encouraged me to start work on this book, and read early drafts of the first chapter. Changes I made as a result of his comments prevented it from digressing into matters of marginal relevance. He also emphasized the importance of giving prominence to 'red blooded' issues, and if the book has this character to any extent, much of the credit goes to Tom. Of course, the views expressed are purely my own.

Extensive material from J. Angelo Corlett's *Responsibility and Punishment* is reproduced with kind permission of Springer Science and Business Media.

An early version of Section 7.2 was presented at the Joint Session of the Mind Association and Aristotelian Society at Aberdeen in July 2008.

I would like to thank Samantha Kirk, Brian DeRocco and Ashley Baird at UPA for speedy answers to my enquiries on various matters, including preparation of the manuscript, making this process considerably less painful than it would otherwise have been.

I would also like to thank my parents for much practical help during the period when this book was written, and I appreciate the support and encouragement I have received from Ian and Jane Munro. My gratitude goes above all to my family: my long-suffering wife, Nimfa; my seven-year-old son, Jonas, who, despite his tender years, has occasionally shown himself a dab hand at fixing the printer; and my twenty-two-month-old daughter, Tanya, for . . . well, just being adorable.

Howard Simmons
Grays, Essex, U.K.
November 2009

CHAPTER ONE
QUANDARIES OF DESERT

1.1   Gary Hart and the Selby Rail Disaster

In February 2001, a man named Gary Hart was driving along an English motorway. In circumstances that are a matter of some dispute, his vehicle came off the road, careered down an embankment and ended up on railway tracks. A passenger train collided with it and was then pushed into the path of a goods train travelling in the opposite direction. The accident caused the deaths of ten people. Gary Hart was convicted of causing death by dangerous driving and sentenced to five years in jail (www.BBCnews.bbc.co.uk/1/hi/england/1754336.stm).

The prosecution maintained that Hart had fallen asleep at the wheel. He denied this, but it was concluded that tiredness had been a crucial factor in the cause of the accident. Hart had apparently spent the whole of the previous night chatting on the phone to his new girlfriend, whom he had met on the Internet.

The most obvious victims in this situation were the ten deceased and the injured, but some would argue that Hart himself was a victim of injustice. He had not intentionally done anything heinous. A freak combination of circumstances turned what would normally have been regarded as no more than mildly imprudent behavior into the cause of an exceptional disaster. Mildly imprudent behavior should not attract a five-year prison sentence. Every one of us is mildly imprudent from time to time, but few of us actually end up doing great harm either to ourselves or to others as a result. It seems that Hart was just extraordinarily unlucky. No doubt the relatives of the deceased would find this hard to accept. Taking their side for a moment, we might question the implicit assumption that bad luck can never render someone culpable. But we need to analyse the situation more carefully if we are to reach a confident judgement. Doing so will, I think, help us to clarify some important aspects of our thinking on the subject of desert.

In U.K. law at that time, the maximum sentence for causing death by dangerous driving was imprisonment for ten years, while that for dangerous driving alone was imprisonment for two years. (Since then, the former has been increased to fourteen years. Such discrepancies in sentencing are found in most jurisdictions.) So Hart's sentence obviously did not exceed what the law permitted—indeed, it was much less. However, the disparity in the maximum sentences for the two offences can be questioned from a moral stance. As the case showed in a very dramatic way, whether one has merely driven dangerously or driven dangerously and thereby killed can be due merely to luck, over which, by definition, one has no control. A person who drives dangerously, but is lucky enough not to end up killing anyone is treated much more leniently than someone who drives equally dangerously, but who, through massive ill fortune, does kill someone. It is highly plausible to claim that this is a morally unfair difference in treatment.

But the unfairness owed to disparity of treatment alone will not actually take us very far in deciding what should be done in cases of this kind. In order to equalize, should we be more lenient with dangerous drivers who kill or harsher with those who don't? We need further moral intuitions for guidance here.

Perhaps a hint is to be found in my reference to Hart's *intentions*. I pointed out that he did not intend to do anything heinous. We could argue that, irrespective of how the consequences turn out, punishment is inappropriate if the offender did not intend anything bad to happen. According to this view, Hart should not have been punished at all.

But this suggestion is too simple. Lawyers talk about *mens rea* (literally a 'guilty mind') as the basis of criminal responsibility. *Intention* to do harm is certainly one form of *mens rea*, but there are two other standardly recognized forms, namely *recklessness* and *negligence*. Are either of these relevant to the present case?

Recklessness means knowing that one's actions will or might do harm, but not caring about this, or not caring enough. It could be said about Hart that, though he did not intend to kill anyone, he did know that his actions might do harm and did not care enough to act differently. Is this plausible, given the agreed facts of the case? After his car had careered onto the railway tracks, Hart made a genuine attempt to prevent disaster, including alerting the emergency services. It is evident, then, that when he knew the danger, he cared greatly about saving lives. In response to this, it might be said that though the greatest danger existed after the car had gone onto the tracks, there was danger in his driving prior to that point. (The charge was after all causing death by dangerous *driving*.) His indifference on the latter score was what constituted his recklessness, according to this argument.

However, this is not at all plausible if we accept the prosecution's contention that Hart had fallen asleep at the wheel. If this was what happened, then at the moment the vehicle was starting to go down the embankment, he could not have been aware of what was happening. It is possible, of course, that somewhat earlier, he may have started to become aware that he was falling asleep and chose not to do what is generally recommended in such a situation, which is to stop and take a rest. And what is even more plausible to suppose is that, during the previous night, he had consciously chosen to continue chatting to his girlfriend on the phone instead of going to bed, thus creating the state of drowsiness in the first place. So for these reasons, wasn't Hart guilty of extreme recklessness, justifying a severe prison sentence?

Actually, this is not so clear. While it *might* be true that just expecting that one will be acting in a potentially harmful way, as opposed to *intending* to act harmfully, is sufficient for deserving some sort of punishment, we need to ensure that the punishment is proportionate to the offence. More specifically, this means that the punishment deserved by the agent should be proportionate to the degree of *expected* harm that he knew or believed was involved in his actions. The probability of killing ten people if one is in a state of drowsiness while driving and one does not take a rest, though not zero, is quite small. (The same point applies even more undeniably to the act of continuing to chat on the phone instead of going to bed.) Creating a very small danger of something terrible happening is not anywhere near as bad as creating a certainty of that thing's happening. Indeed, it is impossible to live a normal human life without creating such risks. So it does not seem right to say that Hart deserved a severe penalty for this form of *mens rea* either.

So finally let's consider the last of the three standardly recognized forms of *mens rea*, criminal negligence. This is held to apply in cases where, although the offender may not have believed that he was doing anything wrong, any *reasonable person* would have realized this. According to this view, one can be rendered culpable, and thus deserving of some sort of penalty, not because one actually believed one was doing harm, but because one *would* have believed this if one had been a reasonable person. One can apply this hypothetically to Hart if one supposes, for example, that he had somehow missed all the warnings about driving while sleepy. One can concede that his ignorance on this matter implies that he was not aware of the dangers, but still hold him to the standards appropriate to someone who was not thus ignorant. Of course, this line would still be vulnerable to the objection that the expected harmfulness of driving while sleepy is much less than the expected harmfulness of an act of deliberate killing. Therefore, it will still not support the harsh sentence passed on Gary Hart. But it is interesting to ask whether the idea of desert based on criminal negligence is a plausible one anyway.

It is hard to see that it is. If an agent is not aware of something that 'any reasonable person' would believe, then he is *ipso facto* not a reasonable person. In that case, why should he be held to account for not doing what a reasonable person would do? To suppose that he should is tantamount to blaming someone for his stupidity or ignorance, and this surely cannot be morally justified, especially if it results in significant distress for the person blamed. Of course, most people do have opportunities from time to time to improve their knowledge and understanding, and sometimes they could be held to account for failing to make use of these opportunities. But surely this should affect only what they deserve for their poor responses to such particular opportunities on the occasions that they are provided with them, not what they deserve for later lapses that may have been caused by those responses.[1] And as a purely practical matter, it would usually be rather difficult for judicial authorities to trace such lapses to actual instances of choosing to be ignorant. How would anyone go about tracing the source of Hart's (hypothetical) lack of awareness of the dangers of driving while sleepy and therefore of establishing that this source lay in specific decisions to remain ignorant?

In summary, of the three forms of *mens rea*—intention, recklessness and negligence—only recklessness is clearly attributable to Gary Hart and that only to a small degree. An injustice was certainly done, at least in so far as justice is a matter of moral desert. But what theoretical conception of deserved punishment is presupposed by this conclusion and can it be defended?

1.2 Internalism versus externalism

There are many different kinds of desert claims.[2] Some of them seem to be intimately connected to morality, but perhaps not all. If a military officer says 'Watkins deserves to be demoted,' does he necessarily make a moral claim? Perhaps he only means something like 'From a military viewpoint, Watkins deserves to be demoted.' A military viewpoint may not be a moral viewpoint because the conclusions drawn in it may not be answerable to the sorts of demands that we associate with morality. After all, it might be said, armies are there to fight wars, not to cultivate virtue. Against this, one could argue that if the officer did not think that Watkins ought to be demoted from a moral viewpoint, then he did not *really* think that the officer ought to be demoted—real desert, it might be claimed, is moral desert, for morality reigns supreme. I do not want to resolve this issue here, merely to separate out types of desert claim that are not relevant to my concerns, namely those that need not be viewed as being based on morality. There are also some forms of desert that seem to be morally relevant, but which are still not of the sort that concerns me at present. An example would be: 'Jim deserves compassion because his young daughter has just died, and for no other reason' (Feldman 1997, 183). At present, I am dealing specifically with claims about what a person deserves that are directly based on an assessment, whether comprehensive or partial, of that person's actions or attributes from a moral viewpoint. This is often called *moral appraisal*.[3]

In my analysis of the Gary Hart case, I concluded that Hart was culpable, at most, for mild recklessness, in that he did certain things, such as not taking enough sleep and continuing to drive while sleepy, which he may have realized were potentially harmful or dangerous. The fact that through massive bad luck, these actions resulted in disaster was not his intention and he could not have been expected to foresee it (except perhaps as an extremely slight possibility), and so the occurrence of the disaster ought not to be considered as increasing his culpability. We might say that this analysis of Hart's case suggests that culpability or desert[4] is 'in the head' or, in other words, 'It's the thought that counts.' In fact, according to one view of the nature of desert, we can leave out actual events altogether. Judith Jarvis Thomson proposes the principle that 'whatever we do, our doing of it is no more to our discredit than are those purely mental acts by which we do it' (1993, 199). This view is called *internalism* and contrasted with *externalism*, according to which desert must depend at least to some degree on realities beyond the mind of the agent.

Peter French challenges the internalist position (2001, 183). In support of his view, he asks us to imagine an individual in a virtual world (perhaps one created by a very sophisticated computer simulation) who believes that he is murdering someone. He has all the mental states associated with committing a real murder, but no person actually dies. French asks if we would describe such an individual as an 'evil-doer.' He thinks we would not (though he concedes that we might consider him dangerous or as having a 'bad character'[5]). Evil, for him, is not just 'in the head'; it depends crucially on real people being harmed. The lesson to be learned in respect of desert, according to French, is that what actually happens to real victims is a crucial element in determining what offenders deserve. It is not entirely surprising that French should take this view, since, as we shall see later (see below, Sec 3.3), he conceives of punishment as vengeance. (It is difficult to take seriously the idea of avenging a 'virtual crime.')

I have to say that consideration of French's thought experiment inclines me to the opposite of his view. Granted, we would be unwilling to describe the virtual killer as an 'evil-doer.' We tend to think of 'doing evil' as consisting at least partly in the physical execution of certain sorts of acts, but this person is merely having certain thoughts and making certain illusory 'decisions.' However, what I think is crucial here is the assumption that the virtual reality simulation is sufficiently complete to deprive him of the knowledge that he is not in fact doing anybody any harm. He *believes* that he is killing someone. Surely, granted this assumption, such a person deserves the same as someone who really kills, all other things being equal. Admittedly, if the thought experiment involved the agent's being in some sort of psychologically altered state, not thinking rationally or making decisions that are out of character, we might feel differently. As it is, we are to assume that he is his normal self, deliberating rationally, but massively deluded about what is happening. That seems to leave him worthy of blame for the decisions that he makes, despite the fact that these decisions have no effect in the real world.

If this is right, deserving punishment does not require a real victim. When there is a victim, her actual experience is not directly relevant to determining the offender's degree of desert. It is true of course that what happens to the victim as well as other factors (such as the presence of a possible motive) typically help us to make plausible inferences about the offender's mental state, which in turn enable us to determine his level of desert. But to accept this is precisely to concede that the mental state itself is more fundamental. French complains that this view makes the actual victim 'morally immaterial' (185). This is surely overstating things. Victims are important. In particular, how well or badly they cope with their victimization is of direct concern to the rest of society, and may rightfully prompt a highly supportive response. But it does not follow that the victim and her *actual* experience are relevant to the specific issue of what the offender deserves. In particular, an offender cannot reasonably be blamed for the suffering he causes his victim if this is different from the suffering he *thought* he was causing.

Some say that the virtual killer does deserve something, but that it is condemnation or censure, rather than punishment, as the latter should have no application in the area of private thoughts.[6] But for my present purposes the distinction between censure and punishment is irrelevant. What is important here is that both are unpleasant things that people are sometimes thought to deserve. The question is whether the virtual killer deserves something equivalent in unpleasantness to what the real murderer deserves. And I have seen no reason so far to doubt that he does. I should add, however, that I do not necessarily think that virtual killers (if any exist) should be punished. There may very well be reasons unrelated to desert for *not* punishing them (perhaps that it would be a bad idea to grant the state such power in relation to the private thoughts of individuals). I repeat: it is *the unpleasantness that people do or do not deserve* that is my concern here.

A plausible suggestion to make at this point is as follows. If a person believed he was doing X and X was or would have been wrong then he deserves something unpleasant to happen to him, whether or not he really was doing X. For example, if a person pressed a button and he thought that in doing so he was killing someone, then he deserves something bad to happen to him because of this, even if pressing the button had no such effect. Note that it seems that an *intention* to do wrong is not needed for the desert claim to be true. Even if his *aim* was not to kill, he still deserves the unpleasant thing as long as he thought that in pressing the button he was killing. (On the other hand, if his *aim* was to kill, we might argue that he would deserve something *more* unpleasant than if he merely thought he was killing.) In contrast to this, if a person did X, which was wrong, but he did not believe he was doing X or that he might be doing X, then there is no reason to suppose that he deserves anything unpleasant. In the present case, this implies that if he pressed the button and this in fact led to someone's death, but he did not believe that it would or that it might, he does not deserve anything unpleasant. Of course, it is the crucial role that this view gives to the agent's mental states, in particular to his beliefs, that makes this an internalist view.

1.3 Further development of internalism

How far should the internalist approach be taken? What if the agent believed he was killing innocent people, but did not believe, as most of us do, that killing innocent people is morally wrong? An example of this might be a suicide bomber who honestly believes that he is morally obliged to kill himself and various others in the service of what he regards as a 'great cause.' Since he is 'conscientiously' following his moral beliefs, shouldn't he be regarded as blameless and hence as not deserving unpleasant treatment (Zimmerman 1988, 75-6)? It is in the spirit of internalism and a natural extension of the previous arguments to suppose this. And if we accept this view, we will say that desert of unpleasant treatment requires, not only a belief about what sort of thing it was that the agent was doing, but also a belief that, in doing that sort of thing, she was behaving in a morally wrong way.

However, when we start to consider *knowledge*, as opposed to mere belief, an interesting complication emerges. Knowledge requires belief, but it also requires (amongst other things) that the relevant belief be *true*. (For example, we do not say of anyone that he *knows* that he has a brother unless he does have a brother.) When we say that desert requires that the agent believe his action to be morally wrong, must we go further and say also that it requires him to *know* this? What this principally comes down to is whether his belief has to be true. Suppose someone believes that premarital sex is wrong, but engages in it anyway, as his desire is very strong (though still *possible* to resist). Assume also that premarital sex is *not* in fact wrong. Does this person deserve something unpleasant, even if it is only criticism for some sort of hypocrisy? The answer seems not to be straightforward. To my mind, he deserves criticism in one respect, because he did what he himself believed to be wrong but, in the main, he does *not* deserve criticism, because premarital sex is not in fact wrong. This seems to represent a partial retreat from internalism, since deservingness is now seen to depend at least partly on something beyond the agent's mind, namely the moral facts.[7] But because we also seem to want to say that the agent still deserves criticism in one respect for doing what he believes to be wrong, we have a strange *mixture* of internalism and externalism that may prove hard to justify.

Another factor related to the mental state of the agent is mental *difficulty* in doing what he believes to be right. I am referring to such phenomena as 'weakness of will,' where the agent is able to identify what he thinks is the right thing to do, but is unable to bring himself to do it. I believe that mental difficulty, to the extent that it is present, reduces an agent's desert of unpleasant treatment if he does wrong.[8] To be clearer, it reduces the severity of what he deserves by way of criticism or punishment. Two arguments may be offered for this, one intuitive, the other more conceptual.

The intuitive argument proceeds by way of an example. Suppose *A* and *B* are tempted to embezzle some money, but *A* is tempted more strongly than *B*. Both succumb. In all other relevant respects, *A*'s and *B*'s situations are the same. Although *A* and *B* act equally wrongly in a purely 'external' sense, it is plausible to suppose that *A* is less blameworthy than *B* and hence deserves less by way of criticism or punishment. Because she was more greatly tempted, *A* had more to contend with in trying to do the right thing. It would therefore seem unfair for her to be penalized as heavily as *B*.

The more conceptual argument is this. Suppose agents sometimes find themselves in a position where it is mentally *impossible* to do the right thing. Then surely such agents cannot be considered to deserve anything for doing the wrong thing. This seems as incontrovertible as in the case where the impossibility is physical in origin. (I do not deserve anything for failing to act like Superman when people are in trouble.) Now, suppose an agent finds himself in a position in which it is almost, but not quite, mentally impossible for him to avoid doing something which he knows to be very harmful. It would seem strange to say that such an agent deserves a penalty as severe as he would if he found it easy to avoid doing this. It would constitute a strange discontinuity, a violent jump from a state of deserving nothing to one of deserving something very bad with only a marginal difference in the agent's mental state. Surely it makes more sense to say that a marginal decrease in difficulty (from a position of maximum difficulty i.e. impossibility) should create only a marginal increase (from nothing) in the severity of what the agent deserves. But this argument can clearly be extended. Any further small decrease in difficulty should result only in a small increase in the severity of what is deserved. There should be no point at which the severity jumps from a certain level to a level massively greater. But to say this is to admit that deservingness of unpleasant treatment increases gradually with gradual decreases in mental difficulty with respect to avoiding wrong behavior.

We have seen in this and the previous section several ways in which what a person deserves seems to depend on his mental state at the relevant time. Of course, the law often does take account of a person's mental state when trying to establish culpability and hence deservingness. We have already looked at the concept of *mens rea* and how it attempts to encapsulate the relevant mental factors. But what we have seen in this section is that an agent's deservingness can depend on his mental state in two further ways that go beyond the traditional notion of *mens rea*, namely his beliefs about what morality requires and the degree of mental difficulty he experiences if he tries to do what he believes to be the right thing. This considerable dependence on mental states has the overall effect of making desert hard to establish in practice, since we cannot directly observe what other agents think or feel and our inferences in this matter are often shaky. Perhaps we get it wrong more often than we think.

1.4 Further problems with desert

Consider the following thought experiment. An agent A performs many wicked actions throughout the course of her life and is punished for each of them proportionately. Another agent B performs rather fewer wicked actions of similar levels of wickedness to A and is punished for *these* proportionately. So far, it seems each agent got what she deserved. But now suppose we look at the situation more closely and we find that A actually had considerably more *opportunities* to be wicked than B (perhaps because she found herself in more tempting situations or maybe she just lived longer). Suppose also that had B lived as long as A and been subjected to a similar frequency of temptation, she would have performed *more* wicked acts than A. If we know this, our attitudes to A and B may change somewhat. We may start to think that B is a worse person than A. We may also think that A was rather unlucky and that for this reason she should not be punished more severely than B—if anything, it is B who should have suffered more. The actual punishments inflicted on these individuals have been affected by factors that must depend to a significant extent upon chance (length of life and frequency of opportunities to do wrong), and this seems rather unfair, in something like the way it seemed unfair for Gary Hart to be punished more severely than someone who showed the same degree of recklessness as him, but was fortunate enough not to kill anyone. The Hart case, when suitably generalized, suggested that we should look only at an agent's decision—a mental process—in order to determine deservingness (the ensuing events being irrelevant in themselves). The above thought experiment suggests an even more radical stance—that we should look, not just at the actual decisions of agents, but at the decisions they *would* have taken if circumstances had been different i.e. at their *dispositions* to act in certain ways, irrespective of what actually happens.[9]

It is also possible to find some intuitive support for this view by looking at the importance of *character* in our moral assessment of others. If we think that a person's action is a reflection of her true character, as opposed to being something she did 'out of character,' this may make us feel more judgmental towards her and hence perhaps to favour her being more harshly criticized or punished. Assuming that our feelings are not misguided in this matter, it seems to follow that it is primarily a person's character that we condemn and that her acts (even her mental acts) are condemned only secondarily as indications of her character. But to say this is surely to concede the prime importance of dispositions, for to say that a person has a bad character is more-or-less to say that she is *disposed* to act in bad ways under certain sorts of circumstances, not necessarily that she *will* act in those ways—for it may happen that she never finds herself in such circumstances. (In a similar way, a person can be *brave*, without ever having an opportunity to demonstrate her bravery.)

It is, however, quite hard to know how far we should take this. Thomas Nagel gives the example of someone who would have become a concentration camp guard in Nazi Germany if he had not left the country for business reasons in 1930 and subsequently gone on to live a quiet and harmless life in Argentina. Does such a person deserve the condemnation or punishment that is thought appropriate for an *actual* concentration camp guard? Surely not. As observed above, in an extreme case, we could be dealing with someone who has a bad character trait, but who is *never* put in a situation where she can manifest it—for example, someone with a bullying mentality who is always held in subservient positions and as a consequence never actually gets to do any bullying. Does such a person deserve to be judged as harshly as an 'active' bully? It would seem extraordinary to say so, and yet here again we have a situation in which a person escapes the normal burden of judgement merely because of luck.

One can have doubts even about the coherence of the view under consideration. At any given time there are infinitely many ways in which circumstances could have been different from the way they actually are at that time. In unfathomably many of these circumstances, I would have behaved badly (if only because they would have involved my being a different sort of person). Am I to be held responsible for all of these merely *potential* acts of wickedness? Does this even make sense?

Clearly desert theorists[10] need some way of avoiding such absurdities, while giving at least some credence to the intuition that the moral significance of bad dispositions may not be purely a function of the badness of the acts in which they are manifested—or else explaining away that intuition in a convincing manner. I shall not discuss whether this is possible; I merely note it as a further problem for desert theory.

Another argument seems even more awkward for desert theorists, and I shall now introduce it and deal with it at some length. It has been noted before, but perhaps not taken as seriously by desert theorists as it should have been.[11] I call it the *problem of superfluous suffering*. Suppose we have determined that the correct punishment for a certain offence involves a certain level of suffering S. But suppose also that a particular perpetrator of this offence happens to have already suffered S. Then shouldn't this offender be spared S on this occasion? If not, it would seem that he is being doubly punished. Of course, it might be that on another previous occasion he also committed the same offence or another for which S is deemed appropriate, in which case the prior instance of suffering X would have already matched a prior offence and so there might be no danger of double punishment after all. This suggests that we need a more accurate statement of our concern here.

I shall use the term *retributive balance* to refer to the degree to which a person's moral goodness or badness over his entire life is 'well matched' with the happiness or suffering that he experiences throughout the course of that life. There may be no exact measure of retributive balance, even in principle, for there may be no way of exactly measuring either moral goodness or badness, on the one hand, or happiness or suffering, on the other. But there do seem to be clear cases. For example, if a person is very wicked throughout all or almost all his life, and his life is almost unremittingly miserable, then this person has a very 'good' retributive balance. If another person shows the same level of badness throughout his life, but is almost always blissfully happy, then he has a very 'poor' retributive balance.[12] We can now more accurately state the concern that was loosely described above. It is that someone may be 'duly and correctly' punished for an offence, with the result that his retributive balance is actually made *worse* rather than better, because the punishment is unnecessary (from the point of view of desert), given what he suffers over his *entire* life. I call the suffering that such a punishment involves *superfluous* suffering.

One type of situation in which superfluous suffering occurs is that in which we punish an offender who has already 'suffered enough.' To some extent, the importance of this kind of superfluous suffering is already recognized in our judicial practice, when an offender sentenced to a custodial penalty has the time already spent in custody subtracted from her total sentence, only having to serve the remainder. However, if we really take superfluous suffering seriously, we should go further than this. For example, we should also take into account (a) suffering that does not result from punishment; (b) suffering that the offender experienced before the offence was committed and (c) suffering that she will experience anyway in the event that we do not now punish her. (Of course, in all these cases, we would need to consider whether the suffering in question was or was not sufficiently balanced by other wrongdoing.)

These suggestions are likely to encounter considerable skepticism, especially in the case where we are being asked to abstain from punishing because of suffering already experienced prior to the offence in question. For this would seem to imply that it could be right to punish an offender *before* he has committed the offence.[13] To see why, note that if suffering experienced before the committal of an offence could balance that offence, then, if one happened to know in advance that the offence was going to be committed, it would surely be in order to *bring about* the suffering at the earlier time as a punishment. Yet clearly, accepted judicial practice does not allow 'advance punishment.'

Now I would not wish to argue that the desert theorist is committed to accepting advance punishment in practice. For there may be good practical reasons for not allowing it: for example, that it would be all too easy to make mistakes in predicting the crimes that people are going to commit. But it seems to me that desert theorists must allow that advance punishment is right in principle. For consider the implications of the following fundamental conceptual point about desert: the fact that what one deserves for doing something can never be neutral from one's own point of view. It must always be such that one would either experience it as something good or as something bad. This, I think, applies to absolutely all forms of desert, not just the type based on moral appraisal.[14] At any rate, it certainly applies to the latter. Now, it is evident that *punishment*, as a matter of practical necessity, will often involve factors that the offender will not experience as bad. If, for example, the punishment involves being detained in one prison rather than another, and there is nothing to choose between these two prisons in terms of the harshness of their regimes, then the fact of this punishment's being in that particular prison is not a factor that the offender will experience as bad. All such factors are *extraneous* to what the offender deserves, strictly construed. What he deserves, strictly construed, consists only in aspects that he experiences as bad. Now another aspect of a punishment which, in and of itself, is not experienced as bad by the offender is the time at which it occurs, and more particularly the fact of its coming before or after the offence or contemporaneously with it.[15] It is, therefore, irrelevant to what the offender deserves, strictly construed. Hence, if a punishment occurs before the offence,[16] this is, in and of itself, irrelevant to its being deserved by the offender for that offence.

I doubt that many desert theorists would be happy with this conclusion. They might worry that if it were accepted, criminals could justly claim the right to commit crimes because they had unbalanced suffering to 'use up.' But perhaps this can be treated as a *reductio ad absurdum* of the very idea of using desert as the basis for justified punishment. Desert theorists therefore need to say more if their approach is to be considered defensible.

George Sher describes a possible way out for the desert theorist (Sher 1987, 83-5). He agrees that time of occurrence is not important in itself, but argues that an offender's earlier burden cannot balance his later offence because these two things would be measured on different scales with no known 'conversion rate' between them. (The two scales are said to be *incommensurable*.) 'Conversion' between the two is impossible, Sher thinks, because the benefit of the offence is a matter of the freedom that the offender grants himself by violating a moral rule (which is itself a matter of the seriousness of the moral rule, in Sher's view), and such freedom cannot be weighed on the same scales as the unhappiness or frustration of desire involved in the offender's earlier burden, as lack of freedom is a fundamentally different sort of thing from unhappiness or frustration of desire. As these are incommensurable, it does not even make sense to try and match them. In contrast, Sher believes that the offender's benefit *is* commensurable with punishment as conventionally understood, since the latter involves loss of freedom that can be matched with the gain in freedom enjoyed by the offender in violating the relevant moral rule.

Now it should be noted that Sher is not actually concerned here with 'retributive balance,' as I have defined that term. Rather, he is concerned with 'diachronic fairness,' which is a matter of ensuring (roughly speaking) that people's illegitimately gained benefits are matched or compensated by suitable burdens at other times. This is why he talks about the *benefit* of the offence to the offender, a concept for which we have so far had no use. However, one can argue that, irrespective of what role diachronic fairness may play in just punishment, someone who takes desert seriously is simply not in a position to ignore superfluous suffering. An essential ingredient of punishment is suffering, experiencing things badly. If, at any time prior to his offence, the offender suffers exactly what he deserves for that offence and he does not commit any other offence for which he would deserve that suffering, then it does seem that to punish him after the offence is to *over*-punish him. He could justly feel aggrieved in such a case. What would—or at least should—fundamentally concern him is not how much freedom he loses in being punished, but how badly he experiences the punishment.[17]

Of course, if we *were* to take superfluous suffering seriously, there would be grave practical problems. How could we possibly get all the information we needed about the past suffering of offenders, not to mention the suffering they *would* experience if they were not punished?[18,19] Notice that it is not just a question here of finding out the bare facts of what happened to the offender, but also how he subjectively *experienced* these things—how much they made him suffer. In general, this is surely impossible. Perhaps when we are dealing with very severe punishments, those that cause a great deal of long-lasting suffering, it could be assumed that in most cases the offender would not have experienced anything like it before and would be unlikely to experience it if he were not punished. Or perhaps, if there was evidence in some cases that this assumption was false (and that the offender had not done anything else to deserve such a penalty), his sentence could be reduced accordingly. In fact, the problem of superfluous suffering is actually at its most intense, not in this sort of case, but in the case of mild punishments—fines, community service, short custodial sentences and so on. In the case of such punishments there is *no possibility* of reliably determining whether or not the offender's previous experiences or his future experiences if he is not punished are such as to make the proposed punishment a source of superfluous suffering. What we would need to know in principle cannot be known in practice. The same point applies to the minor criticisms and informal sanctions that we inflict on one another in the course of our everyday non-judicial lives.

The point being argued here may nevertheless seem incredible. Surely, it will be said, we can sometimes know that Fred, say, deserves to be criticized because he upset Bert. I agree that, for all that we have seen so far, there is a sense in which we can know this. That sense is a purely *relative* one. Relative to the fact that Fred upset Bert, we might say, he deserves to be criticized. However, there is also an absolute sense of deservingness which takes account of the retributive balance of an individual, which (by definition) concerns the individual's *entire* life. Furthermore, it is surely this sort of absolute desert that ultimately matters, not relative desert. This is precisely because the former takes account of superfluous suffering, whose neglect would, on a desert-theoretic view, be unjust—or so, at any rate, I have argued.

1.5 Positive desert

We tend to think that if people do good things, i.e., if their actions are morally admirable in a way that goes beyond mere avoidance of what is morally wrong, they deserve praise or, in outstanding cases, public honour or recognition. To what extent is this sort of desert—positive desert, as it is normally called—affected by the same problems that we have seen to bedevil negative desert i.e. desert of unpleasant treatment?

Actions that possess a quality of moral goodness going beyond the mere avoidance of moral wrongness are often called *supererogatory*. (An example would be an act of generosity performed without any ulterior motive and directed to someone who is owed nothing.) One might be tempted to think that it is *only* supererogatory acts that should give rise to positive desert for their agents. It is 'expected' of people that (all other things being equal) they will desist from acts of deceit, cruelty and so on. They are thought to deserve criticism or punishment for doing these things, but not praise or reward for *not* doing them. However, there are exceptions to this. Someone who finds herself confronted by an unusually high degree of temptation, which she nevertheless resists, can be considered to deserve praise for holding firm. (Janet has an intense dislike of Pete, but when provided with a perfect opportunity to hurt his feelings, resists the temptation, to her great credit.) So our conception of positive desert needs to recognize both kinds of cases—the supererogatory *and* the non-supererogatory involving resistance to temptation. Actually, they are not as different as they seem at first sight. Both involve rising above a certain standard. In the case of the former, the standard involved is that applicable to agents acting under normal circumstances; in the case of the latter, it is a special (lower) standard, geared to the unusually great temptation that the agent faces.

We saw earlier that doing wrong, and hence (according to desert theory) deserving criticism or punishment, is not dependent on intending to do something contrary to morality, but only requires the agent to *believe* (or possibly *know*—we could not fully resolve this) that her action would be of a type that is contrary to morality. An evil motivation, though it may increase the culpability of the agent, is not necessary for there to be *any* culpability. Does a parallel point apply to positive desert? Let us confine ourselves initially to the case of supererogatory desert. Is it the case (roughly speaking) that to merit praise, it is sufficient to believe that one is doing good or must one additionally intend or be motivated to do good?

The answer is clear. We do *not* generally think that a person deserves any praise for doing what he believes to be good if we think that he is not motivated to do good. For example, just thinking that one's actions will be helping others is not enough to merit praise, if one's motive for doing them is only to advance one's own interests. The chair of a large and highly successful pharmaceutical company whose drugs improve the quality of life for many people is not thought to deserve moral praise for this if his only motive is profit-making.[20]

What of non-supererogatory positive desert? Here the contrast between a belief-driven and a motivation-driven basis for desert does not really apply. For in this kind of case, the agent receives credit for resisting a temptation or provocation. This implies that she recognizes the act as one of the morally wrong types. It also implies that she chooses not to do it *because* it belongs to one of those types. So from the very nature of the case, the agent must have the relevant belief *and* the relevant intention.

But there is a more problematic issue waiting to be addressed here—one that also arose very forcefully in relation to negative desert. Are the purely mental states or acts that we have so far mentioned in relation to positive desert *sufficient* for praise or reward to be deserved? We could imagine a virtuous equivalent of French's virtual killer, who is undergoing an elaborate illusion of being able to perform good acts and chooses to do so for no ulterior purpose. We assume that the agent's personality and character are the same while undergoing the virtual reality experience as before and after. Surely this agent deserves credit for the choices he makes—just as much credit, in fact, as one who makes the same choices in the real world and thus does 'real good.' So it seems that the existence of a real beneficiary is not necessary for deserving praise or reward.[21] This may be a surprising conclusion, and doubtless one that some will find difficult to accept. But I suggest that it is a conclusion with which most who consider the thought experiment carefully will concur.

Because internalism seems to be as plausible for positive as for negative desert, our knowledge of the former is seen to be similarly indirect and our assessments of it subject to a similar degree of unreliability. There are also analogues for some of the other points raised about negative desert in the previous section. For example, there is the difficulty about determining the importance of dispositions as opposed to actions in assessing how much an agent positively deserves. (Does an agent who is very generously disposed but rarely has an opportunity to act generously positively deserve as much as an agent who is no more generous in disposition but has many more opportunities to show his dispositional generosity?) And there is also a problem of superfluous happiness to mirror the problem of superfluous suffering. When we reward a person for some good action, it may be that his retributive balance gets worse rather than better, because the additional happiness created by the reward is inappropriate given the bad things he has done on other occasions or the happiness he has already enjoyed. However, it must be conceded that all these points are less serious in their consequences than the parallel points concerning negative desert. When we are in error in supposing that a person deserves criticism or punishment, the result is that we will be disposed, erroneously, to allow that person to experience one or both of these unpleasant modes of treatment. This is a moral cost. (I assume that it is morally wrong to treat people unpleasantly without justification.) In contrast, there need not be any moral cost in giving someone praise or reward that she does not deserve.[22]

In the next chapter, however, we examine an argument that has been used to show, not merely that it is extraordinarily hard to know what people deserve (positively or negatively), but that in fact we can know that they never deserve anything.

NOTES

1. Holly Smith has argued that the relationship between the earlier neglectful acts or omissions and the subsequent lapses is analogous to that between an act or decision that risks harm and the subsequent harmful event that may or may not occur (Smith 1983). Whether the agent is blameworthy for the later lapses in the former case therefore resolves itself into the question (already raised here in effect in my fourth paragraph) of whether the actual occurrence of a harmful event adds to the blameworthiness of the risky decision that led to it. Smith leaves the answer to this open. I claim that it does not, a position which I defend in the next section.

2. Sher (1987, 6-7) provides an impressive array of examples.

3. I am also limiting myself for the moment to claims of *negative* desert, i.e., claims about unpleasant things that people deserve, as opposed to claims of *positive* desert, i.e., claims about deserving pleasant things—benefits—of some sort. Positive desert is discussed at the end of this chapter. (See below, Sec. 1.5.)

4. I shall treat the two terms 'culpability' and 'desert,' where the latter refers to negative desert, as interchangeable.

5. That we might blame the agent for a character flaw is also mentioned by Leo Zaibert when considering a similar thought experiment (Zaibert 2005, 138).

6. This line of argument was suggested to me by Tom Sorell.

7. Some philosophers find the notion of a 'moral fact' problematic. They think that morality is a matter of attitude or stance rather than of truth-evaluable fact. (See e.g., Ayer 1946, 102-113; Blackburn 1984, 181-202.) I am not intending to commit myself one way or the other on this question. Along with Blackburn and others, however, I do regard it as legitimate at least to talk *as if there were* moral facts. Indeed, if this is not granted, it is hard to see how applied ethics is possible at all.

8. See Zimmerman (1988, 104-106) for a defence of the contrary view.

9. Several authors have defended this view, e.g., Rescher (1993), Richards (1993) and Zimmerman (1993).

10. By 'desert theorists,' I mean those who attach a fundamental importance within morality to considerations of desert. I reserve the term 'retributivism' for the theory of *punishment*, which says that punishment is morally acceptable if and only if it is deserved.

11. Two writers who *have* taken it seriously are Ezorsky (1972b—one of the best introductions to the philosophy of punishment that I know) and Zimmerman (1988, 170-171).

12. For the purposes of this broad-brush account, we need not concern ourselves with the extent to which a measure of 'badness' should incorporate dispositional facts like those discussed above.

13. This is different from the argument that is sometimes heard for preemptively 'punishing' individuals who, it is thought, are likely to be threats in the future, e.g., by confining them in secure accommodation. Such action aims to *prevent* the crime in question. In terms of the current argument, this sort of pre-emptive action (if successful) would have no justification, for then the suffering might not be balanced by any later offence—unless (recalling the idea of dispositional desert above) one were to regard the fact of the agent's being dangerous as itself a piece of wickedness that needs to be balanced by suffering.

14. Apparent exceptions turn out to be spurious, I think. One is illustrated by 'She deserves neither happiness nor suffering, so she deserves a life that is neutral in those terms.' This is really a case of *non*-desert. The last clause is merely repeating the information that the person does not deserve happiness and does not deserve suffering. Another type of case is provided by figurative uses as in 'This book deserves more attention than it gets.' But even here it seems that what is deserved is being regarded as a metaphorical benefit.

15. Of course, there can be *consequences* of the time of occurrence that the offender experiences as bad, but that is a different matter. The time itself is never experienced as bad. But suppose someone has an (irrational?) tendency to feel mental anguish *simply* at the fact that something is happening *at 3 p.m.* This is still not a counter-example, as what the person would be experiencing as bad would be his *being under the impression* that the thing was happening at 3 p.m., not the objective fact of its happening then. According to those who take desert seriously, he might deserve to be under that impression, but he would not, strictly speaking, deserve the objective fact itself. Indeed, it is nonsensical to suppose that people can deserve objective facts as opposed to subjective states of one kind or another. And this itself follows from the fact that everything deserved must be experienced as either good or bad by the person who deserves it.

16. I am assuming, of course, that it is *conceptually possible* for a punishment to be inflicted before the relevant offence. Some might maintain that '*A* was punished for the burglary he committed before he even committed it' is a logical contradiction. Though odd, I do not myself find it to be self-contradictory. In any case, nothing turns on this. The real point is that the idea of superfluous suffering, in the sense understood here, entails that suffering can be deserved in virtue of an offence that it precedes in time.

17. Of course, he will probably experience the loss of freedom badly in two respects: (a) he will simply find the thought of it unpleasant; and (b) it will remove opportunities that he might otherwise have had to rid himself of other bad experiences. Loss of freedom is important, then, but only as a contribution to the badness of the experience in general.

18. Joel Feinberg appeals to this sort of consideration in objecting to the aim of 'match[ing] off moral gravity and pain' (Feinberg 1970, 116). But he does not conclude from this that we ought to abandon the attempt to find out what people deserve. Rather, he thinks that we should conceive of deserved punishment differently, in terms of society's need to condemn serious moral wrongs. My view is that the idea of retributive balance is too essential to our concept of desert (at least implicitly) to permit the retention of the latter without the former.

19. We would also need to know in detail about all the other misdeeds (and virtuous acts) of offenders throughout their lives, including the future. This boggles the mind.

20. The explanation for this difference may be that when someone is inclined to do something bad, we want them to be discouraged from doing it and criticism or punishment can be good tools for achieving this, whereas if someone has an independent reason for doing a good thing, she may need no further encouragement to do it.

21. We do tend to think that if someone tries to help another, but fails through no fault of her own, she deserves at least some praise for the effort. What is unexpected is the conclusion that she deserves no *more* praise if she actually succeeds, and that it does not even matter whether the intended beneficiary actually exists or is just a delusion.

22. But see below, Sec. 6.1 (second bullet point).

CHAPTER TWO
THE IMPLICATIONS OF DETERMINISM

2.1 Determinism, 'hard' and 'soft'

Recall the situation of Gary Hart. Many of the events leading to the Selby Rail Disaster were beyond Hart's immediate control. These included the descent of the car down the embankment before he was alert enough to do anything about it and the arrival of two trains at the precise times that they did. Nevertheless, we would naturally say that other parts of the causal chain, such as his decision to stay up throughout the previous night and his decision to carry on driving instead of taking a rest at a crucial time (if indeed he did make such a decision), *were* under his control because they were free choices—he could have chosen differently. I have argued that the badness of these choices, considered independently of their freakish and terrible results, was not in itself very great, and therefore that Hart did not deserve to be treated very harshly and certainly not *more* harshly than someone else who made similar choices without such terrible results. But there is another thought that we may have at this point, which might be considered to excuse Hart completely. The decisions that he made were brought about by events in his brain and the brain is a biological machine. It works (scientists tell us) according to natural laws over which we, the possessors of our brains, have no control. Consequently, our decisions, though they may seem to us to be free, are actually not so, and we cannot be blamed for them. To suppose this is to take a stand on the time-honored problem of *determinism* versus *free will* ('determinism' being the theory according to which all our actions are machine-like in the way explained above). If we accept the determinist view, we seem to reach a very radical conclusion: that we can all avoid blameworthiness or 'moral responsibility' for anything we do.

Philosophers, mostly anxious to protect our freedom and moral responsibility from the threat apparently posed by determinism, have traditionally tended to react to it in one of two ways. They have either tried to explain how we are not, contrary to what science might seem to indicate, really the helpless slaves of natural law, that we have a special status as unique entities of a certain sort, *selves* endowed with free will (*libertarianism*), or else they have conceded to the determinist that we *are* fully part of the natural scheme of things, but that, if we think it through carefully, we will see that this does not in fact entail that we lack free will and hence responsibility for our choices (a view called *compatibilism*, because it says that determinism and free will are compatible with one another). This second response generates the idea that we have free will even though determinism is true, a view often referred to as *soft* determinism. In contrast, someone who adopts determinism and, because of this, rejects free will, is called a *hard* determinist. (Such a theorist is an *incompatibilist*, because he denies the compatibility of determinism with free will.)

But is determinism (hard or soft) true anyway? That is to say, is it the case that everything that exists, including human beings, is entirely controlled by natural laws? Some scientists and philosophers of science regard this claim as a throwback to an outmoded mechanistic view of the world, which twentieth century physics, more particularly quantum theory, has managed to supersede. Quantum theory appears to indicate that at the microscopic level—below the size of atoms—there is a great deal of pure randomness, a lack of predictability that cannot be overcome even in principle. Thus, even if we *are* fully part of the natural world, it does not necessarily follow that our actions are fully determined.

However, we should not be too hasty in trying to use quantum theory to defend moral responsibility. While there may indeed be some indeterminacy at the subatomic level, it appears that this indeterminacy largely disappears when we reach the level of neuron firings in the causation of human actions. It is true that there would not be one hundred per cent deterministic causation under this hypothesis, but there *would* be something only a little short of that, which would imply that whenever we act badly, it would have been very nearly impossible for us to have acted differently and this, by the arguments of Section 1.3, would surely render us very nearly as undeserving of criticism or punishment as we would have been if it had been *totally* impossible. In view of this consideration, it is helpful to use the word 'determinism' to refer, not only to the theory according to which we are absolutely one hundred per cent determined, but also to theories that allow the extent of our being determined to be a little less than this, but still enough to deprive us, for all practical purposes, of moral responsibility and desert.

There is another important point that is often made in this debate. It is that even a high degree of indeterminacy does not in itself entail free will. A highly indeterminate event is one whose causation involves a great degree of randomness. How could the presence of such randomness guarantee a meaningful sort of freedom, the sort of freedom that could, in particular, justifiably attract unpleasant treatment due to those of our actions that turn out badly? On the contrary, it would appear inimical to such freedom.

Before considering this matter further, I shall look at what has proved in recent years to be a more popular approach to the free will problem: the development of a coherent compatibilist view.

Compatibilists argue that even if determinism is true, we can still be free with respect to some of our actions and hence morally answerable for them. What does it mean to say that I am *not* free to do something? In the simplest case, it only means that it is not physically possible for me to do it. For example, I am not free to travel at the speed of light. But clearly, I can also be said not to be free to do some things that it is physically possible for me to do. For example, I am not free to withhold my taxes from the state. This sense of freedom means lack of coercion—I am free to the extent that I am not coerced. Now, it is clear that I can be physically able to do something and not coerced with respect to it, irrespective of whether my action is mechanistically determined. So perhaps simply defining freedom as physical ability plus lack of coercion is enough to get us round the problem of determinism. This was the form mainly taken by compatibilism prior to the late twentieth century.[1]

But the proposed definition is inadequate. There are many kinds of cases in which people are physically able to do things and uncoerced with respect to them, though it is doubtful that they are *free* in relation to them. These include cases of psychological compulsion, brainwashing and hypnosis. In such cases we can argue that the agents involved have been robbed of their ability to do what it is normally in their power to do (or robbed of their ability to avoid doing what it is normally in their power to avoid doing), but there is no physical inability and no coercion in the ordinary sense of the word. It would seem quite wrong to hold such individuals accountable for the actions that they perform in such states, to suppose that they deserve any criticism or penalty in the case where those actions are undesirable.

In order to deal with this, compatibilists have had to devise a more refined conception of freedom. A popular approach makes appeal to the idea of critically or rationally deliberating either about one's possible actions themselves or about the basic desires or evaluations that tend to motivate them.[2] At a first approximation, perhaps we are free (and hence morally responsible and fit objects of praise or blame) to the extent that we are able to engage in such deliberation or reflection. Does this draw the boundary between responsible and non-responsible agents in the right place? Brainwashed agents do seem to be incapable of rational deliberation concerning the actions which their brainwashing seems to render unfree. But in the case of other conditions, such as psychological compulsion and perhaps hypnosis, the problem seems to be not so much the inability to deliberate rationally as the inability to let the results of such deliberation determine one's actions, owing to the fact that the condition itself determines them instead. So it seems that if the compatibilist is going to use the idea of rational deliberation to define a concept of free or responsible action that will rule out agents that are subject to these and similar conditions, she will need to require that an action taken freely and responsibly must be one such that the agent is able to let rational deliberation affect (or totally determine?) the decision as to whether to do it.[3]

But there is a serious problem with this condition of responsible action. Suppose *A* is able to let rational deliberation affect his decisions, but decides not to. This could be either because he does not engage in such deliberation or because he does so, but chooses to ignore what it tells him to do. Then (as Bruce Waller points out[4]) isn't it likely that this fact about A is simply the result of some aspect of A's personality that is due to some combination of genetic and environmental influences? For example, it could reflect a dislike of the process of deliberating which is itself caused by past experience of poor performance in this area due to limited cognitive ability. If, as a result of all this, A chooses to perform a bad action when better deliberation would have prevented him from doing this, is it really right to hold him responsible? It seems that the suggested compatibilist move has deprived determinism of none of its sting, but on the contrary, focused attention on certain—perhaps unsuspected—ways in which its conception of human beings can be brought to bear so as to throw doubt on their free will and capacity for moral responsibility.

Ted Honderich has argued that the debate between compatibilists and incompatibilists is actually a misguided one, since there are two distinct notions of freedom and hence of moral responsibility and the debate illicitly mixes the two (Honderich 2006, 145-151; 2002, 105-121). A strong notion of freedom (*origination*) requires alternative ways of acting and is therefore incompatible with determinism. A distinct weaker notion (*voluntariness*) merely requires absence of coercion, manipulation and so on, and is therefore quite compatible with determinism. By choosing the appropriate notion of freedom, both sides in the debate can claim victory, but then the debate itself is seen to be an empty one. However, it seems to me that even if—as I am inclined to agree is the case—there are these two notions of freedom, then the incompatibilist does get the better of the argument. For it is open to her to claim that, though we *can* use the word 'free' so as to mean merely 'voluntary' (in Honderich's sense), that kind of freedom is a pale simulacrum of *genuine* freedom, which is origination. For only freedom in the sense of origination can, it seems, ground moral responsibility. It is also noteworthy in the present context that Honderich himself argues that retributivism—the theory that bases justified punishment on desert—requires this strong notion of freedom.[5] So at least as far as *desert* is concerned, Honderich is actually an incompatibilist. And surely he is right to be so. If we are seriously disposed to think that none of us deserves anything for our actions because, owing to determinism, we could not have acted differently (and so did not originate our actions), we are unlikely to alter our view on reflecting that some of these actions of ours are voluntary—for voluntariness simply does not affect the point at issue.

2.2 Frankfurt cases

However, this line of argument—indeed perhaps the whole case for incompatibilism—is based on a particular assumption that can be questioned. The assumption is what Harry Frankfurt calls the 'Principle of Alternate Possibilities' (1969), which states that one is morally responsible for an action only if one could have done otherwise. At first this principle appears difficult to deny. How could one be held responsible for doing something if one was not actually able to do anything else? If the action was a bad one, being held culpable and hence deserving of criticism or punishment under such circumstances would seem unfair and unjust. However, Frankfurt has described certain hypothetical cases in which agents who acted wrongly could not have acted otherwise and yet these agents do seem to be culpable.[6] Here is such a case. (It is actually a slightly more specific version of one presented by Michael Otsuka (1998).

In this example Jones can choose whether or not to kill Smith. If he shows an overall inclination *not* to kill him, then a device implanted in his brain by a neurosurgeon (Black) will detect this and cause him to decide to kill him after all. If, on the other hand, Jones chooses to kill him, then Black will not intervene. Clearly Jones is unable to do anything in this situation other than kill Smith. And yet Jones would surely be culpable in the case where he chooses to kill Smith without Black's having to intervene. The fact that Jones is unable to do anything other than kill Smith does not appear to alter his culpability, contrary to the Principle of Alternate Possibilities. We therefore have a clash between our intuitions in this case and the principle, something which, it is argued, casts considerable doubt on the latter.

Many incompatibilists have been unconvinced by Frankfurt's argument. One strategy for responding is to grant that Jones could not have done otherwise but to claim that the principle of alternate possibilities is too crude a statement of what is required for moral responsibility and blameworthiness. When the correct criterion is in place, according to this view, we can see both why we are still inclined to blame Jones in the case where he chooses to kill Smith (without Black's intervention) and why this inclination can be challenged by determinism. One possible replacement for Frankfurt's principle is this:[7]

Revised Principle of Alternate Possibilities:
One is morally responsible for an action only if one could have had an overall intrinsic inclination to do otherwise.

By an 'intrinsic' inclination, I mean an inclination that genuinely originates in the agent, as opposed to being caused by some unusual manipulative process, such as that brought about by Black in the thought experiment. (It might be hard to spell this out rigorously, but the general idea seems clear enough.)

Using this more sophisticated principle, it is clear that, considerations of determinism aside, Jones can reasonably be blamed for his choice to kill Smith in the case where this choice is not brought about by Black. He can be blamed for this because, determinism aside, he could have had an overall intrinsic inclination not to kill Smith. True, if he had had this overall inclination, he would still have killed Smith, because of Black's machinations. But the (non-actualized) possibility of such an overall inclination is what creates his responsibility. However, when determinism is brought back into play, it can be seen that he should not be blamed after all, since determinism tells us, not only that our possible actions are limited to what we actually do, but also that our possible overall inclinations are limited to what we are actually *inclined* to do.

Could moral responsibility, and hence desert, be saved by denying determinism? Could we plausibly argue that human beings stand at least partly, and in a relevant way, outside of the system of natural laws studied by science? This brings us to an examination of the libertarian view, which maintains precisely that.

2.3   Libertarianism

Libertarianism involves rejection of determinism and therefore acceptance of the idea that we could sometimes have acted differently from the way we do act (and been inclined differently from the way we are inclined). It was remarked above (Sec. 2.1) that such a view is not necessarily as congenial to the idea of freedom as it seems initially, since to say that an action is undetermined seems to be the same as saying that it is to that extent *random* and this appears not to be compatible with any meaningful sort of freedom, nor, presumably, with the culpability of the agent in the case of bad actions. Thus the libertarian faces the challenge, not only of justifying the rejection of determinism, but also of explaining how indeterminacy can be compatible with genuine free will and the legitimacy of holding people responsible for their actions. If the libertarian cannot fulfil both of these demands, then we will have to conclude that the theory is a dead end as a response to the determinist denial of free will and responsibility.

But perhaps the libertarian can find a solution to these problems by a strategy that is based on a distinction between two forms of determinism. We might call these *biological* and *psychological* determinism. When introducing determinism in the opening section of this chapter, it was biological determinism that I alluded to: the idea of the human brain as a biological machine proceeding strictly according to mechanistic laws. Psychological determinism, in contrast to this, is the thesis that human behavior is governed by strict *psychological* laws that talk, not about brain synapses and neural firings, but about such phenomena as beliefs, desires, hopes, fears and so on. The two forms of determinism are not equivalent to one another. Biological determinism might be true when psychological determinism is false, for there might be, so to speak, 'causal slack' at the psychological level but none (or virtually none) at the neural level. The reason for this is that psychological 'laws' tend to be subject to exceptions. One such law is the principle that if A desires S and believes that X is the least costly means for obtaining S, then A will do X. This law is subject to many exceptions, because it often happens that these conditions will be satisfied, yet A does not do X. (Perhaps he suffers from weakness of will.) In view of this, one could indeed argue that psychological laws always provide a certain 'slack' that might be thought to accommodate free decision.

Why is the distinction between the two kinds of determinism important? Because of the following considerations. We said that if biological determinism is denied, then to some extent at least, our actions appear merely *random* and so not subject to any sort of free will worth having. But if we look more closely, we see that it is not just a question of randomness here. It is really a matter of whether we can attribute actions to a *self*. For the self seems to be entirely absent from the brain. Neuroscientists have no use for the concept.[8] Yet it seems essential for our actions to be free in any meaningful sense, and hence for us to be answerable for them, that they be *our* actions, at least partly determined by us—that is, by our 'selves.'[9] If we turn to the psychological realm, in contrast, we find that there is not—indeed cannot be—any elimination of the self. Beliefs and desires have to be the beliefs and desires of *someone*. If there is any indeterminacy of action at the psychological level, then it is presumably attributable to the free, autonomous action of selves or persons—exactly what libertarians seek to substantiate.

On the other hand, the idea of the self as a separate, irreducible entity has met with a great deal of skepticism in the history of this subject. It has been pointed out, for example, that this concept is rather mysterious. After all, selves are not physical bodies (though they 'have' bodies). In fact, they appear to lack spatial location. (We tend to think of them as being 'in the head,' but surely that is just a metaphor.) Can there really be such entities? Another concern about the self in the context of a libertarian theory of free will is the fact that it would apparently need to be the sort of thing that can *cause* things to happen—for how else could we be said to control or determine what we do? Yet it is very difficult to see how something that is itself not physical in nature could cause events in the physical world or interact with them in any way at all (Honderich 2002, 48).

To discuss these difficulties in any depth would take us far away from our central task. But there are a couple of other problems with this proposal for rescuing free will about which I shall briefly comment. The first relates to the distinction we drew between two levels, the psychological and the biological, the first of which allows for selves and the second of which doesn't. It is that just because we seem to have what we want at one level, it does not follow that we can just wish the other level away. The biological (neural) level still exists. Indeed, some would argue that it is the only ultimately 'real' level. If at that level there exist no selves, then (perhaps even irrespective of the extent to which determinism applies there) it would seem that there is, after all, no genuine freedom.

On the other hand, must we be so rigid here? Does there have to be one and only one ultimately real level? Perhaps both levels are real and we should choose pragmatically which to use according to our needs at any given time. As neurologists, we could say that there is no genuine free will and consequently no culpability; but as psychologists, adopting a perspective that is more appropriate for the understanding of 'human' problems, we could say that such freedom and culpability do indeed exist.

However, whatever initial plausibility this answer may have seems to be rendered irrelevant by the more serious second problem, which is the thought that determinism may be true even at the psychological level after all. While it may be the case that familiar 'laws' of psychology are subject to exceptions, we need to be aware of the possibility that the psychological laws we are most familiar with are not the best possible means for predicting and explaining human behavior. *Experimental* psychologists have shown us that our behavior is not always motivated in the ways that we tend to think it is. More sophisticated principles that take account of such findings might be more deterministic than those (tacitly) known to us in 'folk' psychology. If so, they would threaten our freedom and culpability in the familiar way described by hard determinists. And remember that it is not necessary to have *total* determinism for culpability to be significantly threatened. Experimental psychology may eventually furnish us with laws that are sufficiently close to being one hundred per cent deterministic to pose such a threat.

2.4 Determinism and morality

It seems that neither compatibilism nor libertarianism provide a convincing means of avoiding the threat to desert posed by determinism. Our actions are probably determined by circumstances beyond our control to a degree that approximates to one hundred per cent. This being so, it is hard to see how we can consider ourselves deserving of anything when we act either well or badly.

But perhaps the implications of hard determinism are even more radical than this. It has been suggested that this theory threatens morality itself, that the very institution of morality fails any longer to make sense once we suppose that our actions and choices are fully determined, depriving us of moral responsibility for them. We might be able to tolerate a situation in which we no longer regard people as deserving certain treatment on the basis of the moral qualities of their actions or dispositions. (Indeed, I shall argue later that we can and should.) But to lose morality itself is to lose our very subject-matter in this enquiry. Rather more significantly, it would seem to alter something central to the way in which we live our lives. Perhaps this is something which, however good the arguments for it, we *cannot* tolerate.

But *why* exactly would one think that hard determinism threatens morality itself? There seem to be three main possibilities:

1. It may be argued that morality is rendered inoperable without praise and blame, and hard determinism renders the practices of praise and blame inappropriate.
2. It may be argued that morality is undermined by hard determinism because of an incompatibility between the latter and the use of morality to categorize actions as morally right or wrong.
3. It may be argued that if determinism is true then we are not really *persons*, and hence not qualified to be moral beings.

I shall take these in order.

Praise and blame

Although this worry looks to be a real and serious one at first sight, further examination shows it to be baseless. We need to ask two questions. Firstly: is it actually true that morality would be rendered inoperable without praise and blame? And secondly: does hard determinism really make praise and blame inappropriate? I deal with the first question (at least in so far as it concerns blame) in Chapter Seven, but we need not wait for an answer to this in order to respond to the main question of morality's status in a hard deterministic world, for it turns out that this can be resolved by addressing the second question.

Certainly, a little thought will show that hard determinism does not render praise of the agents of good actions inappropriate. At most, it only deprives us of one reason to praise such agents. If it is the case that an agent's being truly morally responsible for a good action counts as a reason for praising him, then, if hard determinism is true, we lose that reason in the case of every such agent. But we may have other reasons for praising such agents. For example, we may take pleasure in giving them the warm and satisfying feelings that praise often causes. Or we may wish to use the promise of praise to encourage further good actions from such agents in the future. Just because we don't have a particular reason to praise, it doesn't automatically follow that it would be *wrong* to praise. And indeed, it seems that it is often not wrong, but rather quite a desirable thing, to praise people for doing good things.

In the case of blame, the argument partly parallels that just given for praise, but has to be developed further. If it is the case that an agent's being truly morally responsible for a bad action counts as a reason for blaming him, then, if hard determinism is true, we lose that reason in the case of every such agent. But again, we may have other reasons for blaming such agents. For example, we may take pleasure in giving them the unpleasant feelings that blame often causes (a vengeful reason). Or we may wish to use the unpleasant prospect of blame to discourage further bad actions from such agents in the future. But there is a difference from the case of praise, which is that we frequently have a reason for *not* blaming that has no parallel for praise, namely that blame is likely to cause unpleasant feelings for the person to whom it is directed and that knowingly causing such feelings is (all other things being equal) a morally bad thing to do. (Note that recognition of this reason can quite consistently occur alongside the reasons *for* blaming—we are only dealing with *presumptive* reasons here.) So we can concede that accepting hard determinism and hence the absence of the responsibility-based reason for blame might force us to reconsider in quite a significant way the balance of reasons for and against blame. We may be left with other reasons for blaming, as indicated above. On the other hand, it is not clear that these always outweigh the reason against it based on the presumptive moral wrongness of bringing about unpleasant feelings.[10]

So the claim that hard determinism makes blame inappropriate so far survives, though in a relatively weak and uncertain form. But there are other problems with this claim, or at least with its intended use here. Though we should accept that blaming someone is presumptively morally wrong, and indeed may sometimes be wrong all things considered, owing to the strength of the moral presumption against it in relation to other relevant considerations, we can hardly use this fact in support of an argument to the effect that hard determinism destroys morality. For firstly, the presumptive immorality is not present in every case—sometimes we know, for one reason or another, that the person being blamed will not in fact have unpleasant feelings. And secondly and more importantly, this use of the idea of the moral inappropriateness of blame as part of an argument to show that hard determinism destroys morality is viciously circular. We cannot coherently claim that (if hard determinism is true) morality is destroyed *and* that this is so for moral reasons!

I am a hard determinist, so I reject the alleged responsibility-based reason for blaming wrongdoers. But I accept that there may sometimes be good reasons for blaming them nonetheless (not the vengeful one, I hasten to add). But there is another side to this, namely the possibility that blame may be generally overrated as a way of responding to wrongdoers. This thought will be developed in Chapter Seven.

'Correct' and 'incorrect'

It is possible to argue that 'ought' implies 'can' and that since, according to determinism, we could never act differently from the way we do act, determinism must entail that every statement asserting that we ought morally to do X is false unless X happens to be what we actually do. But that would seem to entail that we can never truly say that anyone has acted in a morally incorrect way, in which case morality would be deprived of its essential 'critical edge.' This appears to be another way in which acceptance of determinism undermines morality.

In my view, we should not be so ready to accept that 'ought' implies 'can.' Granted, there is something at least very jarring about saying 'You are incapable of doing X, but you still ought to do it.' But this might be evidence, not that 'ought' implies 'can' precisely, but of a weaker principle: 'ought' implies 'apparently can.' What prevents me from coherently telling you that you ought to do X when I know or believe that you are incapable of doing it may merely be my *belief* that you are incapable of doing it. This would not necessarily prevent me from speaking truly if you *are* incapable of doing X, but I happen not to know this. Quite irrespective of the truth of determinism, this is a common situation, for determinists obviously do not assert that we always, or often, know what people's exact capabilities are. According to this view of the matter, it is our familiar ignorance of people's capabilities that creates the possibility of moral appraisal using 'ought' and similar expressions. (See Pereboom 2001, 148.)

However, this does not appear to get the incompatibilist totally off the hook. It still seems true that if determinism is correct, we cannot coherently say of someone whom we know already to have failed to do X that she failed to do what she ought to have done. For to reiterate, determinism entails that she could not have done otherwise and therefore, by the principle that 'ought' implies 'apparently can,' also entails that we cannot truly say that she ought to have done X. However, a lot turns here, I think, on the actual form of expression used. We may be reluctant to say that she *ought* to have acted differently if we think she was incapable of doing so (just as we would be reluctant to say of someone that she ought to have travelled to her meeting at the speed of light), but we may feel less uncomfortable in saying in such a case that she *acted in a morally incorrect way*. What accounts for this difference? I think what explains it is the fact that 'ought not to have done' (and some other expressions, such as 'acted badly') carry at least a slight hint of *blame*, whereas 'acted in a morally incorrect way' is more detached and so less likely to carry any such undertone. But if I am right in this, what we are actually dealing with here is a tension between determinism and the appropriateness of blame and the implication is that the correct operation of morality requires that we are generally entitled to hold those who fall short of morality's requirements responsible for their actions and to blame them for their shortcomings. But this is going back to the first of the three arguments, which we dealt with above.

Personhood

Finally, let us consider the last of the three arguments outlined above, which maintains that since, according to determinism, we are not really persons, but biological machines, we are not qualified to be moral beings if that theory is true. It seems to me that this involves an unwarranted 'high redefinition' of the word 'person.' We can certainly agree that if we define the word 'person' in such a way that a person must have genuine free will, then if determinism is true, none of us are persons. But so what? In order to be moral we do not need to be persons in this demanding sense. We only need to be persons in the everyday sense in which that term is understood. What that everyday sense guarantees in particular is that, at least partially, we are able to understand reasons for actions (including moral reasons) and be influenced by them. This is something that is not true of living creatures that are paradigmatically not persons.

Many people think that it would be very depressing if determinism were true. No doubt this at least partly explains the widespread resistance to the theory, both among philosophers and interested lay people. One hears the complaint that if hard determinism is true, then we are little more than puppets manipulated by forces over which we have no control. While I accept that it is possible to view the matter this way, I think it is also possible to see some comfort in determinism. In particular, reminding ourselves that we do not have ultimate responsibility for our actions should act as a counterweight to pointless feelings of guilt about past acts that we cannot now alter.[11] (Of course, it hardly needs pointing out that such an attitude is quite compatible with taking whatever steps we can to prevent ourselves from behaving similarly in the future.) Doubtless, not everyone will weigh the pros and cons of determinism in the same way as me. But it is worth reminding people that there *are* benefits. It is also worth questioning how important real freedom—the sort ruled out by determinism—is to us. For me, the most important thing is not having this sort of freedom, but achieving whatever specific goals I have in life and that is certainly not ruled out by determinism *per se*.

Determinism is often characterized as the view according to which everything that happens is predictable in principle. I think that this is not quite right,[12] but in any case, determinism certainly does not entail that we have such knowledge or that we are ever likely to. If we did, then life would indeed be pointless, as complete foreknowledge would be incompatible with choice itself, not merely free choice (Ginet 1966, 93). But it is irrational to react to the possibility of determinism as if it entailed this.

The foregoing is far from being a comprehensive treatment of the vast issue of determinism and free will. Such a thing would scarcely be possible, and certainly not within the confines of this book. What I have tried to do is show that an incompatibilist can resist at least some of the major types of stratagems that have been suggested for reconciling the two notions. I have also suggested that libertarianism, which accepts free will partly by denying determinism, is not a convincing solution either.

NOTES

1. See, for example, the section entitled 'Of Liberty and Necessity' in Hume 1955, 90-111, where he identifies free will with the ability to do as one wishes.

2. I present this as an example of the sort of approach usually favored by compatibilists, rather than the precise view of any particular compatibilist.

3. This idea of responsible agency is very similar to John Martin Fischer's principle of *weak reasons-responsiveness* (Fischer 1994, 160-189), though more recently, Fischer has modified his view.

4. Waller 1999. One of the targets of his criticism is Daniel Dennett (1978, 297).

5. Honderich 2006, 159. Strictly speaking, it is not the retributive theory itself which requires the strong notion of freedom, but actual punishment justified retributively. (It is possible to think that if people did exercise strong freedom in behaving badly then they ought to be punished, but deny that they ever do exercise such freedom, and so conclude that such punishment is never justifiable in

practice. See also the discussion of J.A. Corlett's position on this matter, below, Sec. 3.5.)

6. Although such cases have come to be known as 'Frankfurt cases,' Frankfurt himself attributes their discovery and use in undermining the Principle of Alternate Possibilities to Robert Nozick (Frankfurt 1969, 835, n. 2).

7. Another has been developed by Otsuka (1998).

8. I must emphasize that I am dealing with a very low level of explanation here. It is literally the level of neural firings and chemical changes within the brain. At this level no reference to a self, or indeed to any other sort of mental entity, is needed. I am not denying that neuroscientists could have an interest in 'the self,' that they could, for example, seek to explain our 'sense of self.' But in so doing, they would be going beyond neural firings and similar low-level phenomena and encroaching on psychology.

9. The 'disappearance of the self' as a central feature of determinist skepticism concerning common sense beliefs is noted by Nagel (1979, 36), though he does not relate this to any distinction between biological and psychological determinism.

10. There is a different view about the role of responsibility in relation to blame, which is that rather than saying that someone's responsibility for wrongdoing provides people with a reason for blaming her, we should say that it gives them *permission* to blame her when there also exist other independent reasons for blaming (e.g. that blaming will do some good). The idea is that, whatever reasons for blaming there might be, it is not appropriate if the blamee is not morally responsible for some wrongdoing. This suggestion parallels the theory of negative retributivism in relation to punishment, which I discuss in Section 3.6. In that section, I explain why I reject the negative retributivist theory. I would apply similar reasoning to the view being considered here. In any case, the advocate of this view would still have to contend with the argument of the next paragraph.

11. In a similar vein, Honderich argues that if we accept determinism we will be less inclined to hate ourselves when we fail to achieve our goals (Honderich 2002, 129).

12. There is a kind of vicious circle, probably insurmountable, in the idea of an agent's being able to predict her own actions. The situation is analogous to that of an experimenter who cannot avoid interfering with the results of her own

experiment. Of course, another person might be able to predict them, but this would not permit the entire future to be predictable by any *one* person, which appears to be implied by the suggested definition of determinism.

CHAPTER THREE
RETRIBUTIVISM

3.1 Introduction

The purpose of this chapter is to examine a particular theory of punishment in the light of our rather negative findings concerning desert in the previous two chapters. But in order to place the theory alongside its main alternative, I want to begin by looking briefly at the moral issue of punishment in general.

What exactly *is* punishment? I shall use the following working definition. To punish a person A is to inflict on A something that she experiences as unpleasant, because one finds something that she has done or tried to do to be wrong or objectionable in some way.[1] The question of the moral justification of punishment arises because philosophers have not always thought it self-evident that someone who has done something wrong (even with *mens rea*) should have inflicted on her something that she experiences as unpleasant. Isn't this a case of countering evil with more evil? How can morality sanction this?

When discussing the morality of punishment, the focus is usually on punishment by the State. This is reasonable, as in most societies it is only the State that is thought to have the authority to inflict severe punishments on people, and also to have the widest *range* of people on whom it can legitimately inflict punishments. (Families, schools and other similar institutions may only punish those who belong to them.) I shall continue this emphasis here, though I will say a little about punishment within the family in Section 5.6.

One of the most prominent theories of the justification of punishment is the *utilitarian* account. Utilitarianism is a general moral theory that states, roughly, that the aim of morality is to seek the maximum possible level of well-being of people generally (or, in some versions, sentient beings generally). Whatever satisfies this goal is morally right in the utilitarian's view; whatever fails to satisfy it is wrong. Applied to punishment, utilitarianism would entail that it is justified only if it maximizes the well-being of people in general. Utilitarians usually argue that it *is* justified because of its tendency to bring about reduced crime rates, which in turn improves people's well-being in obvious ways.

I shall examine the utilitarian approach later. I mention it here only to contrast it with the actual subject-matter of this chapter, retributivism. To a non-philosopher, it might initially seem strange that anyone would want an alternative to the utilitarian account. To maximize well-being would seem like mere common sense and if (as seems very plausible) punishment can contribute to this, what further justification is needed? But there has always seemed to be a major problem with the utilitarian view, which is this: utilitarians make no direct reference to *desert*. For the utilitarian, only the final result matters, namely that general well-being is maximized. If this could somehow be achieved by punishing *un*deserving people, then utilitarians would have no problem with doing so. This has struck many as unsatisfactory—perhaps a better theory is available or can be developed.

3.2 Retributivism: a first look

The retributivist theory of punishment, put simply, is the theory that punishment is morally justified if and only if it is deserved and that desert is sufficient in itself to justify punishment. Unlike the utilitarian, the retributivist is not primarily interested in the consequences of punishing people. She may believe that punishment can have beneficial consequences for society, but if so, she will not think this the main reason for punishing. The main reason will always be simply to give the offender what she deserves. It is quite clear that this theory does not suffer from the alleged problem noted above with utilitarianism, for it bases the justification of punishment directly on the notion of desert. It remains to be seen whether we will think it convincing overall, especially in view of the sceptical findings of the first two chapters.[2]

Retributivism consists in, or can at least be seen to entail, two theses. The first, called *positive* retributivism, maintains that if someone deserves punishment, she should (all other things being equal) be punished simply in virtue of that fact. The second, called *negative* retributivism, maintains that for someone to be justifiably punished, she must deserve punishment. To put it another way, positive retributivism says that the deserving should be punished (simply in virtue of their deserving punishment), while negative retributivism says that the non-deserving should *not* be punished.[3] What we may call *standard* retributivism combines both theses, but some thinkers are negative retributivists without being positive retributivists.[4] They condemn the punishment of the innocent, but their attitude to the punishment of the guilty is that, if the latter *are* to be punished, it must be on grounds other than mere desert—e.g., prevention of future crimes. (See, for example, Hart 1963.)

The prohibition that negative retributivists place on punishing the innocent is a highly plausible one (though how absolute it should be is another matter[5]). Does its inherent plausibility entail that we are bound to incorporate into our conception of justified punishment an *essential* reference to desert? This question will be considered in the final section of the chapter. First, I shall evaluate positive retributivism.

One preliminary, rather subtle, point. There is a difficulty about the definition of positive retributivism that I gave earlier. I said that according to the positive retributivist, if someone deserves punishment, then she should (all other things being equal) be punished simply in virtue of that fact. The problem with this becomes apparent when we consider how to define desert itself, something we have not so far directly addressed. A very plausible outline definition is this: A deserves X if and only if there is a presumption that A should receive X in virtue of his satisfaction of certain criteria related to his actions/mental states/dispositions.[6] Of course these criteria would then need to be spelt out. Here we could either adopt a superficial approach in terms of conventional ways of assigning positive and negative desert or, if we accept the arguments of Chapter One, a deeper (internalist) approach in terms of mental states only. At present, this aspect of the definition need not concern us. What is important here is the requirement that A deserves X when there is a presumption that A should receive X on the basis of *some* set of criteria. When combined with the definition given for positive retributivism, this gives dubious results. For we would then be defining positive retributivism as the theory which claims that, when there is a presumption that someone should be punished (on the basis of certain criteria), then (all other things being equal) she should be punished simply in virtue of that fact, and this of course is little more than an explanation of what it means to say that there is a presumption that someone should receive certain treatment, and so not a substantive philosophical position at all.

I feel sure that the problem here is not with the suggested definition of desert, which seems to reflect our usage of the term reasonably well, but with my definition of positive retributivism. What alternative definition is there? Well, we could say that the distinctive claim made by positive retributivists is that *many people do deserve punishment*, a proposition not actually entailed by the original definition, as the latter is framed in purely conditional terms. This proposal is not wholly without merit, since it is characteristic of positive retributivists to think that many people do need punishing. However, at least one defender of retributivism (J.A. Corlett, whose views will be discussed below in detail) has stated that the theory requires only the conditional claim that if any wrongdoer does satisfy the conditions for moral responsibility with respect to her wrongful actions, then she should be punished, which does not in itself entail that any wrongdoer ever has satisfied those conditions. So how could we define retributivism in a conditional way without allowing it to collapse into tautology? The answer, I think, is that *for the purposes of defining positive retributivism*, we can define desert *non-normatively*. What this amounts to is that the definition of desert is to be purged of its normal commitment to recognising an obligation to treat people in certain ways when they satisfy the relevant criteria. It will merely specify what these criteria are (as precisely as needed). We will then find that we can retain the original definition of positive retributivism. That is to say, positive retributivism will be defined as the claim that if someone deserves punishment, she should (all other things being equal) be punished simply in virtue of that fact, while for the purposes of this definition only, the concept of A's deserving treatment X will be treated as equivalent to the claim that A satisfies certain criteria (which incidentally have the property that most people believe there to be a presumption that anyone who satisfies them should receive X). Clearly, this explanation of the concept of desert does not commit itself to recognising the existence of such a presumption, and therefore leaves the task of making this commitment to positive retributivism itself. Tautology is avoided.

Because of the pivotal importance that it gives to desert, positive retributivism is, *in practical terms*, rendered dubious by the findings of the preceding two chapters (whether or not it can survive in its purely conditional form). In the first chapter it was shown that it is much harder to establish the truth of desert claims than we normally think, sufficiently hard that at least the 'routine' appeal to desert in moral matters is not feasible. In the second chapter, a more familiar argument was defended to show that in fact no-one ever deserves anything. And there is a further sort of argument that can be advanced—this time effective against the pure conditional form of the theory. A retributivist appears to value the punishment of deserving people in and of itself, and not because it would lead to other consequences that might be thought valuable (e.g. deterring future wrongdoing). But how can suffering be, in and of itself, a good thing? Suffering seems to be the very paradigm of something bad. Some retributivists (such as G.E. Moore) claim that it is not the suffering in itself that is good, but the *complex* consisting of a moral offence plus the suffering of the offender—or at least that it is intrinsically better to have this complex rather than the offence on its own. (One might say that the suffering of the offender 'cancels out' the badness of the offence.') But it still seems to me that the suffering of the offender would just add a further bad thing to the badness of the offence itself. As it is often put, 'Two wrongs don't make a right.' That suffering *in and of itself* improves anything strikes me as an implausible notion.[8]

J.L. Mackie comments on this implausibility in retributive thinking. His view is that the retributive idea is a universal human notion and yet, upon examination, it appears, for the sorts of reasons we have seen, to make no rational sense. The solution to this paradox, according to Mackie, lies in seeing that our idea of desert is not ultimately based on reason, but rather on emotion, on the so-called 'reactive attitudes,'[9] such as anger and hostility. These emotions are, Mackie suggests, grounded in evolutionary biology, since they are biologically useful defences against the threats typically posed to the survival of the species by the uncooperative behavior of some of its members. Once we see such emotions, and the idea of desert itself, in these terms, Mackie thinks the impression of absurdity created by the idea of answering wickedness with the infliction of suffering will be dispelled (Mackie 1985, 206-219).

Mackie's attempt to invoke evolutionary biology to explain the reactive attitudes is interesting, and his suggestion may well be true. However, there is an important objection that may be raised against any attempt to use these observations to *justify* the retributive idea in response to skeptics like myself.[10] Firstly, while the propensity to feel some sort of retaliatory emotion in response to being wronged, or seeing others wronged, does appear to be pretty well universal, it varies a great deal in strength from one individual to another. Those who do not feel it very strongly or persistently may well resist the imposition of retributive norms that do not reflect their own moral intuitions. (Many find that their retributive emotions usually do not persist for long, and that a lack of clear justification tends to accelerate their extinction.) More tellingly, they might ask: is this tendency towards retribution a morally *valid* or acceptable one? Perhaps if it *were* maximally strong in every human being and totally resistant to reason, it would be pointless to ask about its moral validity, for the answer could make no difference to our behavior. But the fact of its variation in strength and persistence, together with its susceptibility to reasoned argument, at least for some individuals, shows that its existence, however deeply it may be rooted in biological terms, does not settle the moral issue.

Another type of attempt to defend the coherence of the retributive idea involves viewing an offence or wrongdoing as a kind of 'disturbance to the moral order,' and conceiving of punishment as a means by which that order can be restored. In Chapter One we saw a theory of this kind from George Sher, who views punishment of offenders as a way of achieving 'diachronic fairness,' whereby their illegitimately gained benefits are matched, or compensated by, suitable burdens at other times. In that chapter we did not evaluate Sher's theory directly, so I propose to do this briefly now.

Sher maintains that an offender always gains a certain sort of benefit from his offending, namely, the freedom that he grants himself in violating a moral rule. Is this plausible? If I violate a moral rule, do I thereby enjoy a sort of freedom? In Chapter Two I endorsed the view that none of us are ever genuinely free in our actions or choices. But perhaps it would be unfair to place very much weight on this here. Perhaps Sher's point could be made in terms of the compatibilist's sense of freedom, involving voluntariness, lack of coercion and freedom from such things as mind-altering drugs, hypnosis etc. It is uncontroversial that offenders often exemplify this weak sort of freedom. However, Sher needs to show more than this. He needs to show that such freedom must be a *benefit* to the offender. However, the offender does not necessarily experience any benefit of freedom in addition to the specific benefit (e.g. possessing stolen goods) that the offence secures him. It is true that he might in some cases experience such an additional benefit. He might enjoy the sense of throwing off moral restraint, which he has perhaps found previously to be oppressive. But this is by no means always the case. Consequently, the essential foundation of Sher's attempt to justify criminal punishment as a means of restoring the moral balance is seen to rest on a flawed assumption.

Another theory of punishment which construes it as a means of moral rebalancing is Jean Hampton's theory (1988, 111-161). Hampton's approach is different from Sher's, in that instead of focusing on the benefit of the crime to the offender, she looks at its implications for the perceived 'relative value' of offender and victim. Specifically, she argues that the offence, in harming and humiliating the victim, makes the false statement that she is less valuable than the offender. Punishment, by 'lowering' the offender so that her actual value relative to the victim is again apparent, demonstrates the real truth that offender and victim are, as persons, of equal value.

We might begin by questioning the latter thesis. Is the commonly held moral view that all persons are of equal value actually correct? I for one do not *intuit* that all persons are of equal value. Rather, I have very different attitudes to different people. I find some people admirable and others contemptible and the majority somewhere in between. It will be claimed that this, though true, is irrelevant. The equal value of all persons is supposed to be an objective moral truth that transcends, in some sense, these purely subjective likes and dislikes. But what happens if we try to be objective? I think we still find inequality. Thus some people are, so to speak, better instruments for the production of what is generally taken to be objective value (moral or otherwise) than others, for they are kinder, cleverer, braver or harder-working, and this would seem to imply that they themselves have greater instrumental value. (Notice that this does not in itself entail that they *deserve* anything.) My opponent will no doubt object that we are supposed to be talking about intrinsic value here, not instrumental value Perhaps people often have intrinsic value in the sense that their lives contain many things of intrinsic value (such as pleasure, knowledge, satisfying relationships with others and so on), but again this clearly leads to *differentiation* in the intrinsic value of people, since some people lead lives containing much more of these things than do others.

I would concede that there is one form of egalitarianism that does seem very plausible. If we consider those aforementioned sorts of things in people's lives that have intrinsic value, we will find it plausible to think that, from a moral perspective, it makes no difference *who* has them. For example, morally speaking, an episode of pleasure or a state of knowing some interesting truth has intrinsic value that is independent of who has it—it is just as intrinsically good in one person as in another. (Similarly, an episode of pain is just as intrinsically bad in one person as in another.) However, this does not establish that persons themselves have equal value, for it does not answer the argument previously given about different amounts of these things in different people's lives.

In view of all this, it is hard to think of any sound basis for the thesis we are considering that does not rest on some very dubious theory to the effect that there is something, a soul perhaps, that all people have, and which constitutes the source of their equal value. Since few beyond the influence of certain religious doctrines would contemplate accepting such a view, I think all that really remains of the thesis is the echo of a politically influential—and perhaps rhetorically useful—doctrine about equal human rights for all.

In case any reader thinks that I have dismissed a whole tradition of ethical thinking far too casually, let us grant, for the sake of argument, that all people *are* of equal value. Does it follow, as Hampton alleges, that the act of harming another requires a punitive response designed to demonstrate this? Hampton argues that the original act of harming creates evidence that the offender is superior in value to the victim—a footnote makes clear that she intends the term 'evidence' to be taken quite literally in this context (Hampton 1988, 129, n. 25).

But is this plausible? If it were so, then whenever anyone committed such an act, rationality would require us to be less confident about the supposed truth of the proposition that all people are of equal value. But surely there is no plausibility in this at all. No-one has ever supposed in any other context that I am aware of that violations of ethical principles should rationally make us less confident of their truth. If that were so, then every murder that is committed ought to make us less confident about the truth of the proposition that murder is wrong, which it certainly does not. Therefore, the fact that acts of harming others occur cannot be regarded as evidence against the equal value thesis and so this cannot be a reason why they should need 'annulling' or 'explaining away.' So, on these grounds also, I cannot regard Hampton's theory as convincing.[11]

What explains the appeal that the idea of moral rebalancing has exercised for so many writers on the subject of punishment? I do not think this is too difficult to fathom. They have (subconsciously perhaps) picked up on the association between punishment and *restitution*. In restitution an individual (or sometimes a group such as a corporation) makes compensation to a party that it has injured in some way. My view of restitution is that it can be a socially useful practice, and that it often 'feels right.' Individuals (we will leave groups aside here for the sake of simplicity) often suffer as a result of injuries inflicted on them by others. We tend to feel in such cases that something ought to be done to reduce their suffering. To do this may require some effort, perhaps undesirable or even painful effort, on someone's part. In the case where the injury was caused by someone satisfying the conditions for *mens rea*, it can then seem natural to lay the burden of such effort on the shoulders of this person, in so far as it is natural—though not, it should be noted, necessarily *correct*—to suppose that she deserves such treatment. So the idea of punishment becomes mixed up with the perceived need to bring the injured party back into a more satisfactory state, to *restore* the status quo. Of course, this would still leave the question of whether, and if so how, punishment that contributes to restitution could be *justified*. But the point is that the justification need not use the same idea of rebalancing that the connection with restitution naturally suggests. In my view, no convincing account of the justification of punishment that does so has been found.

Still, retributivism itself remains a popular theory. I now want to look at two recent accounts, one by Peter French and the other by J. Angelo Corlett, to determine whether they succeed in resolving the problems about desert that we have raised.

3.3   Peter French and vengeance theory

Retributivists are sometimes accused of giving an account of punishment that portrays the latter as pure revenge and hence not worthy of serious moral consideration. A vengeful act of punishment seems to be the very opposite of a morally acceptable response to wrongdoing. The word 'vengeful' implies an action based on anger and a sense of personal injury, not one taken in the light of calm reason and determined objectively. It also conjures up images of uncontrolled vigilantes inflicting punishment without regard to due process of law and hence of the dictates of justice.

Peter French is unusual in being prepared to defend a conception of punishment as a form of vengeance. He does not think that the latter has to have the anarchic and highly undesirable features implied by vigilantism. Indeed, he believes it to be subject to definite rules. His book, *The Virtues of Vengeance*, is a very unusual one in philosophical terms. Before we even get to the philosophy proper, we encounter a very lengthy section discussing depictions of vengeance within literature and film. A whole chapter is devoted to the genre of the Western vengeance movie. He sees in the heroes of such films models of a certain sort of integrity, a sort of 'inner strength' demonstrated through their avenging actions.

Here, in outline, are the main features of French's theory.

French provides a set of conditions (a modified version of some rules devised by Robert Nozick[12]), which he thinks encapsulate the idea of 'virtuous vengeance' (French 2001, 70). Suppose A has carried out an action X and B seeks to avenge it. Then B's revenge will be successful—and virtuous—if:

1. B felt that X, an act that inflicted a harm or injury on someone, possibly B, was, to some degree or extent, wrong,
2. And imposed a penalty on A,
3. That reflected, at the time, how strongly B felt about the wrongness of X,
4. Intending that the penalty be exacted because of the wrong act X,
5. And in virtue of the wrongness of X,
6. Intending that A realize that the penalty was visited on him or her because he or she did X,
7. And in virtue of the wrongness of X,
8. By someone who intended to have the penalty fit and be executed because of the wrongness of X,
9. And who intended that A would understand that the penalty was inflicted on him or her so that 1-9 are satisfied.

One thing worth noticing about these principles is that they construe revenge as a response to the committal of *wrongs*—presumably moral wrongs—and not simply actions of which B has a purely subjective dislike (a point unaffected, I think, by the reference to B's *feelings*). This means that, despite seeing punishment as revenge, French's theory does qualify as a moral theory in some minimal sense.

The inclusion of conditions (6) and (7) suggests that, according to French, successful vengeance requires that the offender come to understand that her act was morally wrong, the infliction of the penalty being the means to achieve this. But that does not seem to be quite what French intends. For he says, in another passage, that it is only the wrongness of the act *as perceived by the avenger* that the offender has to understand (French 2001, 85). It seems to be sufficient for him that the offender come to understand that the avenger thinks the act wrong—it is *not* required for successful vengeance that the offender come to think the avenger is right in her evaluation of the act. French does agree that an improved consciousness of right and wrong on the part of the offender would be a good and desirable thing. But that is not the primary aim of punishment. Despite the misleading impression created by conditions (6) and (7), French does not think that a major goal of punishment is to make the offender a better person. It is certainly French's view that successful punishment as vengeance has to have *some* particular effect on the offender. The effect is that she receives a particular message, specifically that the avenger thinks that what she—the offender—did was wrong and that that is why the avenger is punishing her. We should note that the conditions required by French for justifiable vengeance are reasonably stringent (despite the impression created by the reference to what *B* 'felt' in condition (1)). For example, an avenger is not entitled to punish without adequate evidence of the alleged offender's guilt. If necessary, she must undertake appropriate investigations to establish this (which would include ascertaining whether the offender had *mens rea*).

These, then, are the principal features of French's conception of punishment. But how does he *justify* punishment as vengeance? In fact, he brings forward a range of considerations, though I am not entirely sure in every case that they are really intended as justifications which he hopes will persuade skeptics, or whether they are intended merely to characterize the sort of thinking that tends to accompany and cohere with a belief in the moral desirability of punishment as vengeance. However, I shall treat each consideration as if it were intended as justificatory, on the grounds that any of them might potentially turn out to make a contribution in this regard.

One argument that French offers is that the very notion of a moral code requires the practice of responding in a hostile way to wrongdoing. This argument is best examined in a later chapter, where we look at the question of the relation between morality and blame (Chapter Seven). Leaving this aside, we are left, I believe, with four main considerations.

Honor

French notes that in many cultures in which revenge is regarded as an acceptable response to injury, it is thought to restore the *honor* of the injured party. He regards this as an important aspect of his own conception of punishment as revenge. In fact, he thinks it may be what renders the desire for revenge *rational*. It is not so much that the desire for honor is a rationally based desire in itself. It is rather that, given the fact that people generally do want their honor preserved and that successful revenge is a way of achieving this, the latter can be seen as rational in virtue of securing what people want (French 2001, 93).

Inner strength

I alluded to this idea earlier. It seems to represent a kind of courageous self-reliance that French particularly admires and finds to be morally valuable. In fact, French believes that 'inner strength' is a fundamentally good form of motivation and that 'retributive hatred' is a good motive only in so far as it furthers inner strength (French 2001, 123). He concedes that an ethic of inner strength is not amongst the most benevolent, but thinks that it can ground basic duties of honesty, i.e., avoidance of lying, cheating, stealing etc. His argument for this, which draws on Michael Slote (1995, 90), is that a person who was not honest in this broad sense, but relied on others to be honest, would not be self-reliant and so would lack inner strength (French 2001, 126).

Anger

For French, anger is a key emotion grounding hostility towards wrongdoers:

> If we do not react angrily when our values are attacked, our friends are harmed, our family members are injured or insulted, who are we but, as Aristotle says, slaves without moral fibre? Any moral theory that would counsel total restraint of anger under such circumstances is, in Aristotle's terms, foolish. (French 2001, 94-5)

Anger is often thought to be a destructive emotion. Presumably, French would concede that it can be taken to unjustifiable extremes. What he is attacking is complete restraint of anger in circumstances that can reasonably be thought to warrant this emotion.

Defending the moral order

This idea is rather loosely expressed in various places throughout the book. In a way the previous quotation, with its description of unjustifiably suppressed anger as 'foolish,' seems to imply a warning against a cast of mind or policy that could be said to *endanger* morality. Here are two other quotations that convey this idea more explicitly:

> ... the avenger shoulders the moral duty of empowering what is morally right. (French 2001, 85)

> Wrongful actions require hostile responses. That is the basic form of the rule of retaliation, the principle of positive retribution. That . . . is actually one of the primary foundations of morality. . . . It links our cares, the non-cognitive as-

pects of our moral lives, our expectations and beliefs, and our ideals to action. And because of it vengeance may be a virtue and is sometimes necessary to maintain the moral order. (French 2001, 97)

For French, we, the community, have a duty to punish offenders, since failing to do so would be to endanger morality itself (French 2001, 224). But if for any reason we fail in our duty, individuals are fully entitled to take over and exact vengeance, provided they satisfy the conditions on virtuous vengeance outlined earlier (French 2001, 225).

We have now seen a varied melange of ideas that are all intended in some way to explain or defend (as I have said, it is not always clear which) the idea of justified punishment as virtuous vengeance. What are we to make of them? Are they in fact likely to convince those skeptical of the idea of punishment as vengeance? I shall not attempt an exhaustive critique, but will confine myself to a few limited remarks.

Perhaps the most original contribution is the attempted link between virtuous vengeance and the ideas of inner strength and self-reliance. Certainly one can see how a person might manifest either or both of these in inflicting a retaliatory attack on a wrongdoer. It might be a difficult operation requiring effort and planning; the intended victim might be a powerful individual and the sympathies of others might be with her rather than with the avenger. However, it is unlikely that this fact in itself will do much to persuade anybody who is hostile to the idea of taking vengeance to view the practice more sympathetically. After all, it has to be admitted that it may also require great self-reliance and inner strength to carry through a project—assassination of a popular and democratically elected leader, say—that would be regarded by almost everyone as profoundly immoral.

It also seems correct to say that the idea of anger cannot really do any serious justificatory work within French's system. It can plausibly be maintained that there *are* circumstances in which total restraint of anger, even in response to a grave wrong, is morally necessary. There are circumstances in which showing anger—any anger—would inflame the situation and harm people, including possibly innocent people. Furthermore, most of us would counsel some restraint of anger in many situations, precisely in order to avoid an atmosphere that would be likely to lead to acts of pure vengeance which we consider to be unjustifiable. If the latter stance is wrong, then we need some independent reason for thinking so. A similar point can be made about the idea of *honor*. That is, the thought that preservation of honor may require acts of vengeance might make us feel wary of seeking to preserve honor in every situation, rather than making us look more kindly on acts of vengeance.

As for the various references to the idea of morality's being endangered by wrongdoing and the need for retaliatory punishment to protect it, this is reminiscent of an entirely different theory, namely utilitarianism. When utilitarians try to assess punishment in moral terms, they ask how it will affect general well-being and this would presumably include its effects on the moral order, in so far as the latter is conducive to general well-being. So what *is* the relationship between French's views and utilitarianism? In fact, French explicitly denies a role to utilitarian concerns in justifying a hostile response to wrongdoing (French 2001, 106). His exclusion of the offender's moral improvement from the primary aims of virtuous vengeance accords with this. But how, then, are we to understand his emphasis on the empowering of morality and the protection of the moral order? Wouldn't the moral order be enhanced by the moral improvement of offenders? It needs argument to show that the protection of morality is best served by an approach that favors 'retributive hatred.' French has not supplied this argument. It may be that he wants to relegate concern for consequences to the realm of the 'practical,' as distinct from that of the 'moral,' which he sees as more to do with the cultivation of virtues such as 'inner strength.' But that is a questionable contrast. The effects of policies on people's lives, considered without reference to personal bias—including feelings of hatred—can surely be a matter of morality. For example, it would be morally objectionable to advocate a policy, such as the endorsement of vengeance, if one had good reason to think that it would make society more dangerous overall. French himself *seems* to concede as much when he talks about the importance of protecting morality, apparently as part of the process of morally justifying punishment. But protection of morality is forward-looking: it is about consequences. It thus remains very unclear how exactly French's theory is supposed to relate to utilitarianism, which, in its very definition. bases the moral evaluation of actions and practices on their consequences.

A final question. Is there anything in French's theory that would constitute solutions to the problems about desert raised in my first two chapters? As far as the internalist/externalist debate is concerned, French clearly favors an externalist position, as we saw from the stance he took in relation to his own thought experiment of the virtual killer. His intuitions about this are the opposite of my own internalist ones, though readers will have to make up their own minds. What of the problem of superfluous suffering? This is something which (like most retributivists) he does not consider—remarks about the importance of not over-punishing (French 2001, 225) do not in themselves amount to an awareness of this problem. He does look at the better-known problem of determinism and deals with it by adopting J.M. Fischer's concept of moral responsibility as 'weak reasons-responsiveness.'[13] I argued in Chapter Two that moral responsibility, if it were real, would have to conform to some version of the Principle of Alternate Possibilities (and I gave my preferred version). If I am right, incompatibilism is still a real threat to retributivists, and it cannot be met by adopting an account such as Fischer's.

Quite apart from the issue of determinism (which tends to be a rather divisive one), the theory of punishment as vengeance is one that most ethicists find very hard to accept. I do not see that French has said anything that is likely to change their minds.

3.4   Corlett's account: exposition

Another recent defence of retributivism has been provided by J. Angelo Corlett (2006). Corlett, unlike French, does not write in terms of vengeance, for he maintains that retribution is a concept distinct from vengeance, and a more defensible one.[14] In this section I shall explain the main features of Corlett's theory and, in the next, present a critique of it.

The following extract summarizes some key aspects of Corlett's view:

> The reason why the state ought to punish is because offenders deserve it. [This] means, concisely, that to the extent that an offender is responsible for her offence, she should be punished in proportion to her harm to others. [This] means, generally, that she was at fault in acting, failing to act or attempting to act wrongfully and harm others, and that she has done so intentionally, knowingly and voluntarily. And it is the extent to which she acts in these ways that she may and ought to be punished for her wrongful harm to others. (Corlett 2006, 5)

This extract begins with a version of the distinctive claim of positive retributivism, namely, that state punishment of offenders is justified by the (alleged) fact that they deserve it. Corlett continues by presenting further ideas which, rather than being unique to retributivism, form a part of most theories of punishment that have been proposed. These are: (a) an explanation of the concept of desert in terms of *responsibility*; (b) linked with this, an appeal to the idea of *proportionality* between severity of punishment and gravity of offence (which Corlett relates to the degree of harm to others); and (c) a brief explanation (which Corlett subsequently further develops) of what constitutes harming others in such a way as to satisfy standard conditions of moral responsibility.

According to Corlett, many critics of retributivism have been attacking a 'straw person,' a theory that is so implausible that virtually no-one would actually maintain it. For example, it should not be supposed that, just because retributivists appeal only to desert in the primary justification of punishment, they cannot at any point appeal to 'social utility,' i.e., the beneficial effects of policies and actions on society as a whole. A mixed theory appealing to both desert *and* social utility is, for Corlett, the only sensible option. He gives an example of a situation in which a retributivist can legitimately take into account considerations of social utility (Corlett 2006, 56). Suppose *A* commits a major fraud, which contributes significantly to the virtual collapse of a country's economy, and also causes someone to commit suicide because she has lost all her life savings. Corlett claims that a number of different punishments might be appropriate for this offender in terms of desert (assuming that the conditions of responsibility are satisfied), e.g., capital punishment, life imprisonment without parole and forced unpaid labour in an area where *A* can do society some good and has little chance of harming anyone. Since *any* of these would arguably satisfy the requirements of proportional retributive punishment, it is quite reasonable, Corlett suggests, to choose between them on the basis of social utility, which might favor the last of the three. It is clear, then, that Corlett's theory tries to recognize both retributive and utilitarian considerations, but gives the former the primary role in justification.

My quotation from Corlett drew attention to the idea of proportionality in punishment, the notion that the severity of the punishment needs to be matched to the gravity of the offence. Corlett recognizes that any plausible retributive theory of punishment must give some sort of account of how to carry out this matching—though he notes that this is a problem not unique to retributivism (Corlett 2006, 3). He proposes and defends a series of principles of proportionality, rather than a single principle. By producing such principles, Corlett at least hopes to answer the charge that retributivists have nothing plausible to say about proportional punishment.

Corlett's *Matching Principle of Proportional Punishment* is offered as 'a modification of *lex talionis*' (Corlett 2006, 86), i.e., the principle of an 'eye for an eye and a tooth for a tooth.' It states that 'as far as humanly possible, criminals ought to be punished in ways that match the extent of the amounts of harms that they illicitly wrought on others' (Corlett 2006, 86). Then a further principle introduced by Corlett, called the *Harm-Based Principle of Proportional Punishment*, may be viewed as constituting a kind of elaboration of this idea:

> Punishment is justifiably inflicted on an offender only if it 'weighs' the same for the offender ... as the offence 'weighs' ... to the victim on a scale of suffering, where the victim's weighing of her own suffering ... is not influenced by revenge toward the offender. (Corlett 2006, 92-3)

(Corlett points out that the application of this principle assumes that the offender is morally responsible for his offence.)

Like *Lex Talionis* itself, this principle implies that there is no upper limit on the severity of punishments (at least if there is no upper limit on the gravity of crimes). Whatever suffering a criminal inflicts on others must be matched by the judicial system in its treatment of the criminal. Clearly, this would often require punishments, such as torture, which go far beyond what is (officially at least) considered reasonable in western jurisdictions. Corlett is unworried by this: so much the worse for these jurisdictions, he thinks. In response to the widely supported principle that punishment should never be so severe that it becomes inhumane, he argues that this 'cries out for a supportive argument' (Corlett 2006, 89). When we consider certain cases of vicious criminal conduct resulting in extreme suffering for its victims, our intuitions tell us, he thinks, that the perpetrator(s) ought to suffer to the same degree. The inhumanity argument, he argues, begs the question by assuming that the state's use of proportional punishment in such cases is on a par with the criminal's wrongdoing (Corlett 2006, 89). Some writers, Corlett concedes, have offered more substantive arguments against torture. Thus Jeffrey Reiman, for example, suggests that modern states have a 'duty to act in ways that advance civilization,' and that 'progress in civilization is characterized by a lower tolerance for one's own pain and that suffered by others' (Reiman 1998, 108, quoted by Corlett on p. 140). This seems to imply, remarks Corlett, that certain Latin-American states employing modes of punishment that would not be permitted in the U.S. are uncivilized and such an argument, he says, is ethnocentric and *ad hominem* (Corlett 2006, 141). As we have seen, for Corlett, if an offender actually deserves torture, then torture is what he should get. Reiman's rejection of this is, he thinks, based simply on dogmatism. He tells us:

> The fact that many folk shrink at the very idea of, say, punishing even duly convicted torturers with torture is likely a testimony to the success of certain 'humanitarian' doctrines brainwashing even some intelligent people to turn their backs on corrective justice in the name of 'civilization.' (Corlett 2006, 143)

Corlett's position is actually even closer to traditional *lex talionis* than has so far been suggested.[15] For in addition to the two principles of proportional punishment already quoted, which merely require a match between the *amounts* of suffering experienced by the offender and victim, he also presents a *Punishment-in-Kind Principle of Proportionality*, which requires (or at least permits) an attempt by the state to seek the closest possible resemblance between the kinds of harms experienced by the victim and those inflicted on the offender through punishment (Corlett 2006, 89).

The application of this principle would often create problems. Consider the offence of rape. The idea of giving someone the task of raping a rapist would be morally unconscionable, as Corlett concedes; instead of this, he favors the development of a 'punishment machine,' which would produce in offenders the *sensations* associated with being raped (Corlett 2006, 91-2).

Another form of punishment that many have condemned as inhumane is the death penalty. As might be expected, Corlett shows no hesitancy in endorsing the death penalty for those who (as he would argue) deserve it. One commonly heard reason for opposing the death penalty is the danger of executing innocent people. The need within a state punishment system to protect the innocent has seemed to many to be of much higher priority than the goal of punishing the guilty. Corlett refers here to Blackstone's celebrated principle stating that it is better for ten guilty people to escape justice than for one innocent person to be wrongfully convicted (Blackstone 2008, 278). He suggests that the following would be 'more responsible and morally challenging' than Blackstone's formula: 'It is better that no significant crime shall go unpunished (proportionately) and no innocent person's punishment shall go unpunished or uncompensated than for even one guilty person to escape the clutches of justice for her significant harm to others' (Corlett 2006, 87-8).

Corlett is also concerned with the economic waste incurred by providing what he regards as lavish conditions for brutal offenders duly convicted by the U.S. criminal justice system. He suggests that, in the interests not only of proportional punishment, but also of parsimony, harsh criminals should be subjected to a regime in which they receive 'one meal a day,... minimal health care (if any), no libraries, no sports facilities, no televisions, no computers, no musical instruments or other electronic devices, etc.. . . all the while working them vigorously without any monetary compensation whatsoever, regardless of ethnicity or gender' (Corlett 2006, 80), and that the money saved should be used to benefit other citizens. In response to the concerns that reformers would have regarding such measures, he makes a clarification: he only intends them for the very harshest of criminals, those convicted of rapes, murders, etc., not minor offenders (Corlett 2006, 81)—presumably, though, given the other things he has said about the treatment of the former class of criminals, his first choice for many of them would be torture or capital punishment, rather than the regime just described.

I turn now to a brief exposition of Corlett's views concerning forgiveness and mercy. Corlett distinguishes between *forgiving* and *forgiveness*. The former makes demands only on the person doing the forgiving: she needs to cease resenting the wrongdoer and to communicate to her the fact that she has done so. The latter makes demands, not only on the forgiver, but also on the wrongdoer. In particular, it requires that the wrongdoer make a genuine apology. Corlett lays down stringent conditions on what counts as a genuine apology, including an active commitment to rectifying the wrong. In fact, Corlett tells us that *actual* rectification is a necessary condition of a genuine apology and hence of forgiveness (Corlett 2006, 119-120).

In advocating the use of these criteria, Corlett hopes to remedy what he sees as a regrettable tendency amongst philosophers who have considered this issue to place the moral burden of forgiveness on the victim of wrongdoing instead of on the perpetrator. In a similar vein, Corlett argues that there is never an obligation to forgive a wrongdoer, that forgiveness is *supererogatory*. In other words, to offer it may be morally virtuous, but it always goes beyond what morality strictly requires.

For Corlett, forgiveness is mainly a private matter, not the concern of the state. He denies that the state ever has a duty to forgive offenders. He is also skeptical that it even has a *right* to do so, since, even if the victim has forgiven the offender (and there has been genuine *forgiveness*, involving an apology that meets Corlett's strict criteria), 'blameworthiness persists, and because of this punishment is not somehow, mysteriously, unjustified on moral grounds' (Corlett 2006, 127). But he concedes that further argument might be forthcoming to show that the state does have such a right.

Another aspect of the issue of punishment considered by Corlett is the question of the correct response to wrongdoing by corporations (and other 'collectives'), as opposed to individuals. Collectives are punishable for their acts of wrongdoing, Corlett argues, only if they are morally responsible for those acts. They are morally responsible for them only if they satisfy the same conditions for moral responsibility as individuals are required to satisfy (Corlett 2006, 149). But is it even meaningful to ascribe responsibility to corporations and other collectives? Some would argue that such ascriptions are meaningless, since there is nothing to a corporation 'over and above' the individuals who compose it, and so there is no separate entity to be the bearer of responsibility. However, Corlett argues that even if such a reductionist view is correct, it does not follow that the statements we make about corporations are meaningless: each is true (and therefore meaningful) just in case some equivalent statement (or set of statements) about the individuals composing the corporation is true (Corlett 2006, 167-8).

Of course, even if it is meaningful to attribute responsibility to a corporation, it does not automatically follow that any corporations (as opposed to some of the individuals who compose them) *are* actually responsible for anything that they do. One necessary condition of responsibility, according to Corlett, is that the relevant action should be *intentional*. And he maintains that for the action to be intentional, it must be the case that *every* member of the corporation 'serves as a meaningfully contributory cause of it' (Corlett 2006, 170). In practice, this would require a responsible corporation to have a directly democratic structure. As this is not true of most existing corporations, such a view implies that most would have to be re-organized along such lines before they could be held liable for any of their wrong actions. Additionally, Corlett argues, a 'publicity condition' must be satisfied: those considering joining a corporation would have to be informed that 'each and every one of them will be held accountable . . . for corporate wrongful acts to the extent that she was an intentional agent concerning them' (Corlett 2006, 171).

As he himself recognizes, the stringency of Corlett's conditions for responsibility on the part of corporations and other collectives makes it doubtful that large collectives, such as the U.S. citizenry, can be considered responsible for acts carried out in their name—though some smaller bodies, such as the U.S. Supreme Court Justices may qualify (Corlett 2006, 162-3).

In the last major chapter of his book Corlett makes an impassioned case for Native Americans to be compensated for the atrocities committed against their ancestors by the U.S. government. There are, broadly speaking, two types of things for which compensation seems to be morally required in this case. The first is the unjust acquisition by European settlers of land belonging to Native Americans. The second is acts of killing, injury and torture of Native Americans by European settlers. As far as the first is concerned, the basis of the moral imperative to compensate is, according to Corlett, the 'Principle of Morally Just Acquisitions and Transfers':

> Whatever is acquired or transferred by morally just means is itself morally just; whatever is acquired or transferred by morally unjust means is itself morally unjust. (Corlett 2006, 191)

It is clear from Corlett's use of this principle that we must take it to imply that for someone's possession of something to be morally just, it is not enough that s*he* came by it through a just transfer (gift, sale etc.). It is also necessary, roughly speaking, that the earlier history of that item should involve no unjust transfers. For example, if one U.S. citizen purchases some land in good faith from another, this will not be a just situation if the seller obtained it from Native Americans by force or fraud—as Corlett points out, the law itself does not recognize a person's entitlement to something that she purchased in good faith from someone who stole it (Corlett 2006, 193). This connects to a further point: injustice in acquisitions and transfers may exist without moral liability (Corlett 2006, 196). In the example above, it would be no defence against confiscation of the land from the person who bought it in good faith that she had no part in its original unjust seizure. The Principle of Morally Just Acquisitions and Transfers simply does not allow such a defence. When we turn, on the other hand, to the second category of action for which compensation is sought—acts of killing, injury and torture of Native Americans, things appear to be different. The Principle of Morally Just Acquisitions and Transfers has no application here. Rather, we seem to be in the realm of ordinary morality, where, for punishment to be acceptable, moral responsibility must obtain. In that case, it would seem wrong to impose the burdens of restitution on present-day Americans (and others whose ancestors may have been involved in atrocities against Native Americans). But Corlett appears to think that this *is* acceptable, even morally required. He appeals to the idea of collective responsibility discussed earlier, arguing that U.S. government representatives and those who elect them are 'to some meaningful degree "jointly committed" . . . to the "American way of life"' (Corlett 2006, 194).

Corlett considers several possible methods of achieving morally adequate restitution to Native Americans. He sees no valid reason to reject the strictest option: 'the Complete Restitution of Lands and Compensation for Personal Injuries/Loss of Personal Property' (Corlett 2006, 220). Appealing again to the Principle of Morally Just Acquisitions and Transfers, he states that U.S. citizens are not in a moral position 'to deny the legitimacy of a policy that would place them in economic ruins' (Corlett 2006, 220).

3.5   Corlett's account: critique

Corlett has produced a robust and forthright defence of the retributive theory of punishment. But how convincing is it?

The issue of social utility

As we have seen, Corlett sets great store by the fact that his theory, unlike some other retributive theories, explicitly permits at least some weight to be given to considerations of social utility. He considers this a significant strength, since retributivism has been subject to what he regards as the simplistic accusation of being unable to take account of this factor. But what does the utilitarian element in Corlett's theory actually amount to? As we saw, Corlett illustrates the role social utility can play in determining suitable punishments for offenders by considering a case where it may be used to decide between several different punishments each of which maximally satisfies retributive justice. But this represents a very minimal concession to utilitarians, for it applies only in cases where one cannot decide on purely retributive grounds what the correct punishment of the offender should be. One would have to be extraordinarily hostile to the idea of social utility to want to deny it a role in a case of that sort. There is one other sort of case where Corlett *might* be read as giving a significant role to social utility, but it is not really clear that this is the correct way of interpreting his meaning. He says that a society might be justified in waiving the punishment of minor offences in a situation where resources are stretched and many major offences need punishing (Corlett 2006, 84). But his main worry here seems to be not social utility—the general well-being of citizens—but rather the need to ensure that the worst offences do not go unpunished, which could be regarded as a purely retributive matter. It is true that he speaks in this context of the importance of 'overall efficiency,' but this may just refer to the efficiency of the system of retributive punishment rather than the maximization of general well-being.

I think it can be argued that the minimal weight given by Corlett to social utility has implications which most people would find quite unacceptable. Indeed, such consequences are drawn out by Corlett himself. We saw how he seems prepared to allow many U.S. citizens to fall into a state of economic ruin in order to achieve what he considers to be adequate restitution to Native Americans for wrongs inflicted on their ancestors by European settlers. But surely no-one who takes morality seriously can regard this as acceptable. Quite apart from the suffering of those who find themselves in a state of economic ruin, there is also the likely destabilising effect on U.S. society of the collapse in the fortunes of so many of its citizens. The social upheaval and conflict involved could be of enormous proportions. And it is important to realize that avoiding these consequences by refusing to make reparations at the level favored by Corlett neither entails indifference to the difficulties faced by many Native Americans in the modern U.S., nor an unwillingness to seek a resolution of them. More modest restitution plus other measures might be adequate to the task—or they might at any rate achieve the best that can be achieved, given the need to prevent a society from tearing itself apart. Consequentialist reasoning seems entirely natural here, but Corlett appears perversely determined to avoid it, giving disproportionate weight to justice.[16]

Proportionality and extreme punishments

There is an important consideration that none of Corlett's principles of proportional punishment take into account, something that was raised earlier in this book, namely: the offender's degree of certainty that her act would have harmful consequences. We saw this to be an essential element in the assessment of an offender's degree of 'recklessness,' illustrated by the dramatic example of Gary Hart and the Selby Rail Disaster. In point of fact, Corlett is aware of this issue. In his discussion of responsibility he suggests a 'Scope of Responsibility Principle': 'To the extent that I am responsible for X, and to the extent that I, being a reasonable person can understand, by way of common sense reflection, that X is likely to cause or lead to Y, I am responsible also for Y' (Corlett 2006, 25). A little later he adds that the likelihood of Y's resulting from the agent's performance of X helps determine her level of responsibility.[17] It is to Corlett's credit that he recognizes how responsibility for a harmful outcome can be a matter of degree, and that one of the factors determining this is the probability of its occurring given that the agent acts in the way that she does. However, his principles of proportionality in punishment do not adequately reflect this fact. Admittedly, Corlett does remark of the Harm-Based Principle of Proportional Punishment that its application depends on the conditions of moral responsibility being satisfied by the offender. But to put it that way implies (contrary to Corlett's own opinion quoted above) that responsibility is an all-or-nothing matter. The correct approach would presumably be to formulate the Harm-Based Principle so that it made the suffering it requires for the offender depend, not only on the suffering actually experienced by the victim,[18] but on the levels of suffering that *might* have resulted from the offender's action and their associated probabilities—as well as other factors relevant to the offender's degree of responsibility. Of course, this would have made the principle very unwieldy. However, I think it is worth bearing in mind that a full statement of it (and presumably also of the other principles proposed by Corlett) would certainly require reference to factors of this kind.

I turn now to the question of extreme punishments. Corlett says that the idea that 'inhumane' punishments, such as torture or the death penalty, must be rejected is one that 'cries out for a supportive argument,' and that it begs the question by assuming that the state's use of proportional punishment in such cases is on a par with the criminal's wrongdoing. These remarks illustrate a claim made several times in Corlett's book in one form or another to the effect that proportional retributive punishment has such strong intuitive support that we should always presume it to be correct unless we can see some strong reason against it. But some people's intuitions on this might differ from Corlett's. It is possible to think that rough proportionality is quite reasonable in the sense that, for example, a murderer should receive much worse than a fine, while a shoplifter should not receive ten years in jail, but at the same time repudiate extreme punishments such as torture or the death penalty for any offender. Why should proportionality be a moral absolute? One may, without obvious absurdity and without violence to a general adherence to proportionality, think that no-one—not even a torturer—deserves to be tortured. Alternatively, it is possible to think that torture is deserved in some cases, but should nevertheless not be inflicted. As Jeffrie Murphy points out, 'there is a sense in which it seems that the only punishment adequate for a torturer and mutilator is torture and mutilation, and yet one might well have grave and even final reservations about performing such acts no matter how proportionally appropriate they may seem.'[19] As for the charge of ethnocentricity directed at those who, because they view the avoidance of extreme punishments as a mark of civilization, might be forced to describe certain Latin-American nations as 'uncivilized,' surely it is not being suggested that our moral views have to be constrained so as to avoid giving cultural offence. Wouldn't Corlett himself feel obliged to criticize another culture if its penal practices were, to his way of thinking, excessively lenient? There is no suggestion from Corlett's book that he is a moral relativist. On the contrary, he appears to think that retributive punishment is a moral requirement that is applicable to all human societies.

On another matter, is it really acceptable to advocate that human industry and ingenuity be applied to the task of developing a machine that will create a convincing simulation of being raped, to be used on those convicted of rape, even if there is no independent benefit to be derived from this to anyone, including victims of rape?[20] I have no knock-down argument for a negative answer to this question. But I believe it immoral to advocate such a thing. No doubt Corlett would conclude that I am one of the many victims of brainwashing by 'humanitarian' propaganda.

As for the death penalty, has Corlett succeeded in addressing the widely-felt concerns about the execution of innocent people? Corlett does maintain that if innocent people are punished, this itself requires punishment or compensation in response. In the context of the death penalty we would of course be limited to punishing those responsible for the wrongful execution (assuming that they were genuinely at fault) and possibly compensating other innocent people, such as dependants of the executed person, who may have suffered as a result. We would clearly not be in a position to compensate the executed person herself! This appears to represent a severe limitation in our ability to 'right the wrong' of an unjust execution. Another question that can be raised here is whether compensation to innocent relatives and dependents shouldn't apply for executions *in general*, not just 'wrongful' ones. But then again, how does one realistically compensate someone for her sense of bereavement at the execution of a loved one? Surely retributivists should *waive* the death penalty in cases where a clearly innocent person would suffer profoundly as a result of it—unless they are willing to be accused of treating the punishment of the guilty as intrinsically more important than the sparing of the innocent, a harsh position indeed (and one that re-echoes the original objection to the retributivist defence of the death penalty).

Corlett would probably receive more sympathy for his view concerning 'lavish' living conditions for incarcerated offenders. How can one justify the expense involved when the same resources could be used instead for any of a huge number of worthy projects benefiting innocent people? Indeed, it is not just a question of ensuring that serious offenders are not treated lavishly: how could one even justify spending any money on them at all when one could instead use it to help desperately poor innocent people in various parts of the world? Viewed in this way, the argument leads curiously back to the death penalty.

Execution is probably the cheapest way to deal with serious offenders and though, as we have already seen, it can have its innocent casualties, their suffering might often be less than the suffering relieved by certain alternative uses of the money that it saves. If so, Corlett appears to win out here in a way that seems hard to repudiate even on utilitarian grounds.

Of course, if we take seriously the concerns raised about determinism in Chapter Two, the picture changes. If hard determinism is correct, everyone is 'innocent,' and there is no discriminating in terms of deservingness between the offenders spared execution and the beneficiaries of the alternative programmes. However, this line is not sufficient in itself to defend the view (to which I am sympathetic) that offenders, even serious ones, should not only be allowed to live, but should experience something better than the subsistence conditions so vividly described by Corlett. For it seems to leave us in a position where we have no *more* reason to provide decent living conditions to criminals than we have to help all manner of unfortunate people who, unlike the criminals, would not normally be thought to be our (or our government's) responsibility. However, we shall have to delay further consideration of this matter until I have said more about the theory of punishment I myself favor.

Forgiveness and mercy

Corlett's contrasting use of the words 'forgiving' and 'forgiveness' is strange. He says that forgiveness requires, not just an act of forgiving on the part of the victim of wrongdoing, but also an apology from the wrongdoer. But it is simply not true to say that forgiveness cannot take place in the absence of an apology. I can, for my own reasons, choose to forgive someone who has wronged me even though he has not apologized, and if I have forgiven him, then by definition forgiveness has taken place. Corlett is best understood as making a normative, rather than a linguistic, point. Presumably he is saying that there is something *wrong* with forgiving someone who has not apologized. Perhaps to do so is to make things too easy for the wrongdoer. If so, it is not so much that such forgiving does not constitute forgiveness as that it does not constitute *morally acceptable* forgiveness.

Corlett insists that forgiveness is always supererogatory, never a duty. I wonder whether this really accords with our intuitions (not that the latter should necessarily be considered beyond criticism, of course). Suppose *A* deliberately insults *B* in a very public way, thus inflicting considerable distress on her, but then satisfies all Corlett's conditions for genuine apology, including generous restitution. Her sorrow seems as genuine as one could possibly wish for and it has been demonstrated through practical reparation. Suppose, furthermore, considerable time has now elapsed since the insult was made and *A*'s behavior towards *B* in the intervening time has been exemplary. Are we not at least tempted to say in these circumstances that *B* *ought* to forgive *A*? (Of course, for more serious offences than insults we are much less likely to think that there is an obligation to forgive.)

In any case, Corlett's primary concern is with the state and criminal justice system. But here is an important question that he needs to address. Suppose forgiveness of an offender by his victim has taken place in such a way as to satisfy Corlett's strict standards. This would include adequate rectification and would, in some cases at least, impose quite a significant burden on the offender. It could sometimes happen that this burden is equivalent to what proportional punishment for his offence would require. In that case, wouldn't it be wrong in retributive terms for the state to impose the punishment, given that rectification has already taken place? If this line of thinking is correct, then it is not so easy for Corlett to treat forgiveness as irrelevant to criminal justice. By making the conditions for forgiveness in the sphere of personal morality so demanding, he has described a situation in which it appears that forgiveness will at least on occasion do the criminal justice system's work for it.

Punishment of collectives and reparations

Turning now to the question of the punishment of corporations and other collectives, it is important to consider whether Corlett has correctly assessed the implications of reductionism about collectives. This, it will be recalled, is the highly plausible thesis that there is nothing to a collective over and above its individual members, that any true statement about a collective can be 'translated' into an equivalent statement about the members of the collective. Corlett is surely correct to point out that this view does not entail that statements about collectives are meaningless: on the contrary, it provides an explanation of how their meaning is determined. However, reductionism does affect the debate about collective punishment in a way that Corlett does not appear to have realized. Suppose a collective is said to have acted wrongly and satisfies the conditions of responsibility, such that it is considered punishable for its wrongdoing. Suppose that it is indeed punished. If reductionism is correct, this latter fact about the collective's punishment, like any other fact about it, must just consist in certain facts about one or more members of the collective, presumably that *they* have been punished in certain ways. But if that is the case, why do we have to concern ourselves with punishment of collectives *per se*? Why not simply ask of each relevant *individual* what (if anything) she has done wrong and respond accordingly? The only reason I can think of why this might not be sufficient is that correct punishment of a collective might require the individuals within the collective to be treated in different ways from those dictated by principles of individual punishment. But that would be extremely odd. Consider individuals *A*, *B* and *C*, who are members of some collective. In their respective roles as members of the collective, they each act in wrongful ways and satisfy the normal conditions for individual responsible action, such that punishment for each is (retributively) appropriate. On the basis of these facts we punish them, taking no special account of the fact that they acted as members of the collective. But it could turn out, on the suggestion being considered, that if we *had* considered their actions in this way, we would have been obliged to treat them differently. Now of course, there are ways in which someone's acting as a member of a collective can be relevant to determining how she should be punished. Perhaps her role within the collective gave rise to certain pressures which might create grounds for mitigation, for example. But clearly such considerations can quite easily be accommodated without adopting the idea of the collective itself being punishable. I think the supporter of collective punishment needs to explain what it is about this type of punishment that a purely individual conception of punishment *cannot* accommodate. Until this is done, I believe that we are entitled to reject collective punishment as a redundant notion.

Furthermore, Corlett faces more serious objections than this. One concerns what appears to be an outright contradiction. As we saw, Corlett says that he is doubtful that large collectives, such as the U.S. citizenry, can be considered responsible for acts carried out in their names, since it is doubtful that they satisfy the stringent conditions required for moral responsibility. Yet later he goes on to devote a whole chapter to an uncompromising and detailed defence of the view that U.S. citizens ought to compensate Native Americans for wrongs that they, as a collective, committed against them. Have I read Corlett correctly here? Is it really U.S. citizens, taken collectively, that Corlett deems responsible for wrongs committed against Native Americans? Granted, it is usually to the U.S. government that he attributes this responsibility. But, as Corlett himself recognizes, massive liabilities for the U.S. government will be passed on to the citizenry and, as we have seen, he believes this is acceptable, on the grounds that today's U.S. citizens are responsible for the wrongs done, owing to their 'joint commitment' to the 'American way of life.' So the inconsistency cannot be explained away by appeal to the distinction between the U.S. government and its citizens. Could it be that Corlett's doubts, expressed at the end of his seventh chapter, about whether the U.S. citizenry can be a responsible collective have been assuaged by the time he comes to consider the question of reparations to Native Americans in his ninth chapter? This is not plausible either. The reason given in the earlier chapter for doubting the responsibility of the U.S. citizenry is its frequent ignorance of the details of policies pursued in its name (Corlett 2006, 163). There is no indication in Corlett's later discussions of any second thoughts about this matter, either in general terms or in relation to policies concerning Native Americans. In view of all this, I confess to being unable to interpret Corlett's views on this question without imputing the contradiction described.

Of the two conflicting claims—that the U.S. citizenry ought to be held responsible for the wrongs to Native Americans and that they ought not (the latter implied by his limitations on collective responsibility)—which *should* Corlett affirm? Since we are considering the responsibility of *current* U.S. citizens for historical injustices, we need to bear in mind that individuals cannot be held responsible for policies pursued before they even existed. It may be replied that, even though these individuals did not exist at that time, the political collective did—albeit containing different individuals. Corlett in fact says nothing about the criteria for the continued existence of collectives over time. But by his own principles—which seem reasonable enough—for an individual to be held responsible for a decision taken by a collective of which she is a member, it is required that she '[serve] as a meaningfully contributory cause of it.' This is clearly impossible in relation to decisions taken before the member was even born. Corlett seems to be diverging from his own insistence on direct democracy when he invokes the idea that generations of U.S. citizens have been 'jointly committed' to the 'American way of life.' One can be committed to the 'American way of life' in general terms without approving of everything that past and present U.S. governments have done ostensibly in support of it. As we have seen, Corlett also tries to get mileage out of the fact that his Principle of Just Acquisitions and Transfers makes no reference to moral responsibility. But this principle only applies to seizures of land and property—it does not affect responsibility for atrocities. Of the two contradictory claims, it is therefore the one affirming the responsibility of current U.S. citizens for historical wrongs committed against Native Americans that Corlett should give up, though I suspect that it is rather too dear to his heart for him to do so at all easily.

Treatment of skepticism about desert

What are the implications for Corlett's views of the difficulties raised about desert in the first two chapters of this book? One such difficulty was the problem of superfluous suffering. Like French, Corlett appears to be unaware of the problem, or else does not consider it sufficiently serious to be worth mentioning. Of course, the existence of this problem does not refute retributivism. That it is often very difficult to know whether a seemingly appropriate proportional punishment would improve someone's retributive balance is not inconsistent with the claim that if we ever do know this, then we should inflict the punishment in question. But it does make retributivism very difficult to apply in practice. As we saw, it makes it impossible to be sure that one is punishing less serious offences in a just manner. As far as more serious wrongdoings attracting severe punishments are concerned, it seems incumbent on anyone who takes retributive balance seriously to be prepared to waive punishment in those cases where an offender has already experienced suffering comparable to the proposed punishment and appears never to have done anything else to deserve it. It is not clear whether Corlett would be prepared to sanction this.

What of hard determinism? Corlett contributes an interesting observation about its logical relationship to retributivism. Retributivists believe that anyone who performs a wrong act in such a way that he satisfies the conditions of moral responsibility ought to be punished for doing so. But Corlett points out that to believe this is not necessarily to commit oneself to supposing that anyone ever does act in this way, and therefore that anyone ever ought to be punished in practice. He adds, however, that his theory *is* committed to the proposition that there are 'in all likelihood' some responsible agents (Corlett 2006, 227). Like French, he is inclined to justify this belief in the existence of responsible agency by reference to Fischer-style compatibilism.[21] He also claims that a total denial of moral responsibility would destroy morality altogether (Corlett 2006, 31). But he produces no arguments to support this claim, which, in effect, I considered and rebutted in Section 2.4.

Corlett also argues that we should not accept the claim that we ought not to blame or punish wrongdoers because they are never responsible for their actions, since it implies, by parity of reasoning, that we ought not to praise or reward people for morally *meritorious* acts, which, he says, is counterintuitive (Corlett 2006, 31). But he has overlooked an important asymmetry between the two cases. There is a moral presumption against causing harm or distress to another person. This presumption might be overridden if that other person deserves the harm or distress in virtue of wrongdoing. But if she does not deserve it, then (all other things being equal) one ought not to inflict it on her. There is no parallel presumption against treating people in pleasant ways, and therefore, even if someone does not *deserve* to be praised or rewarded, there is, in general, no reason to conclude that we *ought not* to do so.

In view of these considerations, I find unconvincing Corlett's efforts to show that we should, despite the possibility of determinism, accept the 'common sense' view that people are often morally responsible for the bad things that they do, and hence deserve punishment for them. Another important consideration which Corlett does not mention is something that was pointed out in Section 1.3, the suggestion that we cannot hold someone deserving of blame or punishment if, in performing her bad act, she believed herself to be doing the right thing.[22] This matter is particularly serious for Corlett, because in a separate essay he maintains that Hitler and other inflictors of genocide characteristically believe that what they do is good and right (Corlett 2004, 83). He thinks that this is compatible with regarding them as evil and as having acted in evil ways. But for Corlett, acting in evil ways (with responsibility) entails being punishable. This is yet another difficulty for Corlett that he might find hard to overcome.

3.6 Negative retributivism and some thought experiments

Negative retributivism, it will be recalled, is the thesis that it is morally wrong for the state, or anyone else, to punish an innocent person, a person who does not deserve to be punished. This view seems unquestionably right from an intuitive point of view. However, acceptance of hard determinism casts a new light on it. For according to the hard determinist, no-one deserves to be punished for anything and adding negative retributivism to this thesis generates the conclusion that all punishment is morally wrong. Despite being a hard determinist, I do not accept this view. I think that punishment is sometimes justified by its consequences, a view that I shall defend in the next chapter. This means that I cannot accept negative retributivism. Or rather, it means that I cannot accept it in its most uncompromising form, in which it asserts *all* punishment of innocent people to be morally wrong. It would be open to me to suppose that there is always a moral *presumption* against punishing an innocent person, a presumption that exists *because* of the person's innocence, but one that may be overridden if sufficient reason exists to do so. However, I am not sure that I want to accept even this, for such a position must be considered at least highly misleading in my terms. I believe that there is a moral presumption against inflicting harm or distress on anyone, innocence having no special significance. Innocence does not itself create a presumption against harming, for innocence is simply the lack of any reason, in terms of desert, to harm. Since I believe that such a reason is *always* lacking, it is no more appropriate for me to say that there is a presumption against harming *innocent* people than to say that there is a presumption against harming, say, people who can run a four-minute mile.

However, any such wish to leave considerations of innocence and desert out of the picture altogether may be tested by consideration of scenarios like the following. Let us say that you have to decide whether you are going to save one of two men from suffering, the two men being Adolf Hitler and Raoul Wallenberg (a courageous Swedish diplomat who saved many Jews from the gas chambers and who eventually died in a Soviet prison). The duration and intensity of the suffering will be the same, whichever of them experiences it, and nothing else of significance is affected by the decision. I presume nearly everyone would choose to save Wallenberg. I am no exception. What is the reason? Some might say it is the fact that Hitler deserves to suffer more than Wallenberg, or that Hitler deserves to suffer, but Wallenberg does not. But I do not accept that Hitler deserves to suffer in the sense that there exists a reason, independent of consequences, why Hitler should suffer. So anti-retributivists like me who nevertheless choose Hitler to suffer may, on the face of it, have difficulty explaining our stance.

Let's alter the scenario a little. This time if Hitler is the one who suffers, he will suffer very slightly more than Wallenberg will if *he* suffers. Presumably, most people will still say that we should choose Hitler to suffer. I agree. I would say that the new factor makes the anti-Hitler choice more questionable, but not to a degree significant enough to make me reverse my decision.

But now suppose the scenario is changed again, this time so that if Hitler suffers, he will suffer *much* more than Wallenberg. I suspect the majority of people will still want Hitler to be the one to suffer. But, albeit with some trepidation, I have to express my disagreement with this. The most important consideration for me is that in one possible outcome there is much more suffering going on than in the other. I want to avoid the outcome with much more suffering. It doesn't seem so important that the extra suffering would be happening to Hitler. I share the general opinion that Hitler was a terrible person, but I do not think that making him suffer would in itself be a worthwhile thing to do. (Remember an essential stipulation of the scenario: *nothing else of significance will be affected by the decision.* In the real world this is most unlikely to be true. Indeed, in the real world it could be that Hitler's extra suffering does a lot of good—by serving as a warning to potential future tyrants, say. It was precisely in order to abstract from such possibilities that the scenario was framed as an artificial thought experiment.) I do not feel bothered by the thought that it is Hitler who will be spared some suffering through my decision. On the other hand, I must admit to feeling uncomfortable at the thought that Wallenberg will suffer as a result of something I do (so uncomfortable, in fact, that I am not sure that, in practice, if I were *really* presented with this choice, I wouldn't buckle and follow the majority). I do not like the thought of such a good and likeable person suffering significantly more than he could have, especially through my agency. On the other hand, I am a determinist and do not think that any of the good things Wallenberg did were in any deep sense to his credit, nor do I think that any of the bad things Hitler did were in any deep sense *his* responsibility. Hence I pay attention, not to the alleged moral merits of the two men, but to the amounts of suffering in each outcome. And on this basis, I would choose (or at least I *think* I would choose) the outcome in which Wallenberg suffers. In choosing this option, I am of course following the utilitarian line.

Although I admit to some tendency to wobble in relation to this last case, at least I can claim that my (ideal) choice is consistent with my overall anti-desert stance. This does not apply to my stance regarding the first two scenarios, where perceptions of desert seem to determine my choice. However, I don't agree that there is a real *practical* inconsistency here. I choose to make Hitler suffer in these cases, because I am rationally permitted to. Morality, as I see it, does not require either particular choice on grounds of desert. But even *I* am not one hundred per cent certain of this. For I am not one hundred per cent certain that hard determinism is true. How could I be? Given the immense complexity of the question, as revealed in the preceding chapter (which did not even cover every aspect, only those that seemed to me most salient), and given also the fact that the majority of people, philosophers and non-experts alike, disagree with me, it would be sheer arrogance on my part to claim certainty. This is enough to explain my choice against Hitler in the first two scenarios. In fact, these scenarios have been framed in such a way that even the slightest doubt about the truth of hard determinism and consequent tiny suspicion that the conventional view might be true will, in a rational person, lead to a choice against Hitler.

NOTES

1. The definition does not cover every case that might be labelled 'punishment.' For example, it does not cover cases in which people are 'punished' for what their ancestors have done. It might be argued that such action is indeed punishment even if it is wrong or unjustifiable. To achieve precise necessary and sufficient conditions is probably impossible and certainly not needed here.

2. There are a few other theories of punishment that appear to be neither retributivist nor utilitarian: for example, Herbert Morris' 'consent' theory (1968). This theory and related ones are heavily criticized by Honderich (2006, 48-57). There are also theories that combine elements of both retributivism and utilitarianism, such as R.A. Duff's account, to be discussed in Section 4.2. Coverage of all available theories has not been attempted here.

3. It has been suggested that only the deserving or guilty *can* be punished, since it is part of the definition of punishment that it entails guilt. (If you punish the innocent, what are you punishing them *for*?)—see Quinton 1954. This would appear to make negative retributivism incoherent or at least inappropriate, for how can it make sense to tell us to avoid doing something that we *cannot* do in any case? However, this linguistic claim about the word 'punishment' is only that—linguistic. The substantive question remains unaffected by it: can it ever be right to impose 'hard treatment' on someone who does not satisfy the standard criteria of desert (roughly, committing an offence with *mens rea*)? The negative retributivist's answer to this question is that it cannot (though she may allow exceptions in extreme cases).

4. I do not think, however, that anyone has ever advocated positive retributivism without also accepting negative retributivism; indeed, such a view would scarcely be plausible.

5. In order to be entitled to call himself a negative retributivist, a person must think the prohibition very strong, but presumably need not regard it as absolute.

6. As well as describing the criteria in more detail, a full account would have to refer to the non-neutrality of desert, as explained above, Sec. 1.4.

7. Moore 1993, 262. Interestingly, Moore does *not* think that this applies when the pain is very intense, and he would not therefore regard his conception as justifying extreme punishments such as torture.

8. See Honderich (2006, 28) for an amusing and provocative repudiation of this notion.

9. The term comes from P.F. Strawson's influential essay 'Freedom and Resentment' (1974, 1-25).

10. This was possibly not Mackie's intention. He does not talk about anybody questioning the retributive idea—indeed, as we have seen, he regards it as

universal. However, one can easily appreciate that his arguments *might* be used in this way.

11. Criticisms relating to other aspects of Hampton's theory, particularly those concerning the question of whether it makes sense to suppose that punishment *could* succeed in correcting the false statement of unequal value, may be found in Golash 1994.

12. However, Nozick prefers not to classify punishment as revenge or vengeance. (See Nozick 1981, 363-397 and, for very effective criticisms, Honderich 2006, 176-184.)

13. French 2001, 200-201. See above, Chapter 2, note 3 for a reference to Fischer's theory.

14. Corlett 2006, 2-3. My own view is that, in ordinary usage at least, 'retribution' and 'vengeance' scarcely differ in meaning, though the latter carries with it less desirable associations (that is, less desirable for the majority of professional ethicists).

15. Corlett says that he does not think that retributivism is necessarily *committed* to *lex talionis* (Corlett 2006, 91). But his advocacy of the Punishment-in-Kind Principle shows clearly that he himself favors something very close to it.

16. Corlett might respond that my even-handed approach does not take account of the responsibility in which, as he sees it, even modern U.S. citizens share for the 'American holocaust.' I deal with this point in the sub-section below criticizing Corlett's treatment of the issue of collective punishment.

17. Corlett 2006, 26. Strictly speaking, the concept of likelihood invoked here might not necessarily be the same as the offender's own degree of certainty, for it might be an objective probability, assessed on the basis of evidence to which the offender might not have had access. I ignore this complication in what follows. The distinction relates to the difference between recklessness and negligence, discussed above, Sec. 1.1. A high objective probability of causing harm does not imply recklessness, though it may imply negligence. However, I argued in that section that negligence is not a valid basis for culpability. If this is right, Corlett's proportionality principles need to be framed in terms of subjective probabilities.

18. I argued in Chapter One that the victim's actual level of suffering is not directly relevant to determining the offender's deservingness, but I doubt that

Corlett would accept this, and I am here only discussing what might work in Corlett's own terms.

19. Murphy and Hampton 1988, 107. Murphy goes on to explain a possible reason for this stance: that one's 'retributive hatred' is overcome by one's 'inherent moral decency.'

20. If Corlett were advocating this primarily because he thought that there *was* such a benefit to be derived from it, he would presumably have said so, and his position would be much more utilitarian than we have any reason to think it is.

21. Corlett 2006, 21-2. See also above, Chapter 2, note 3.

22. This point is made in a generally positive review of the book by Ishtiyaque Haji (2002, 849).

CHAPTER FOUR
A UTILITARIAN APPROACH TO PUNISHMENT

4.1 Utilitarianism in general

Having rejected retributivism as a convincing theory of the moral justification of punishment, I turn now to its great rival, utilitarianism. Of course, utilitarianism is not *just* a theory of punishment. It is intended as a comprehensive moral theory, which sees the aim of morality as the maximization of general well-being. Punishment is only one of many practices to which it can be applied. The theory has had some distinguished advocates, but it has also had its philosophical enemies. They have brought against it a range of different objections, some reasonable, others perhaps a little unfair, and defenders of the theory have introduced various refinements to deal with some of the reasonable ones. Punishment itself has been one of the battlegrounds.[1] The others, including some highly abstruse questions regarding the theoretical possibility of measuring well-being and of comparing the levels of well-being of different people, are beyond the scope of this book. Fortunately, it is not necessary here to settle the question of the validity of utilitarianism as a general theory of morality. We are concerned only with the question of whether the utilitarian approach is a feasible option in the case of the problem of punishment (and to some extent in relation to certain other matters in later chapters). If we decide that it is, we are not committed to supposing that the theory gives useful results in other areas of morality. Nor are we committed to supposing that well-being can be measured in a precise way. We assume only that levels of well-being can be approximately estimated. In point of fact, there exist a range of utilitarian theories, which differ in their answers to various questions of detail. I shall only mention differences that seem relevant to the topic of desert or punishment.

But before proceeding to the main business, I want to comment on the use of the term 'utilitarianism' and another related to it, *consequentialism*. This is important, since instead of using the two terms interchangeably as I do, at least one major writer on this subject with a stance very similar to my own—Ted Honderich—distinguishes them. For him, utilitarianism is committed to a quite specific way of evaluating the goodness of an outcome. This is the *aggregative* method. To illustrate it, suppose the population happened to involve just four people and their levels of well-being in a given outcome were represented by the numbers: 5, 10, -3, -4 (higher numbers for greater well-being). Then the overall level of well-being in this outcome would be the sum of these numbers, which equals 8.[2] This is not the only method of evaluation that one might consider using. For example, instead of adding the numbers, one could find their mean. (In this example the latter method would represent the overall level as $8 \div 4 = 2$.) Honderich sees utilitarianism as necessarily aggregative; he would not recognize any of the other methods as constituting a utilitarian theory, strictly understood. He would, however, call them *consequentialist*, since for him consequentialism is simply any moral theory that identifies the rightness of actions or policies with the production of the best possible overall consequences, however 'best possible' may be understood in detail.[3]

Aside from the question of the 'correct' use of words, which is, after all, not a very important one, one might ask which of the various methods of evaluation is substantively correct. In other words, which one correctly characterizes the goodness of outcomes and thus provides (according to utilitarianism) the basis for determining morally correct action? This is not an easy question to answer. But there is at least one reason for thinking that the aggregative method, at any rate, is profoundly unsatisfactory. For suppose it were the case that the only way of relieving a hundred people from a small itch was by torturing one person. Though each small itch counts for very little in terms of well-being, added together they could easily outweigh the agony of the one person's torture, which, on the aggregative theory, entails that we should indeed sacrifice the well-being of the one to ensure the well-being of the many. But this seems intuitively quite wrong. Surely it is much better for the hundred to put up with this tiny itch than for the one to suffer agony. This strongly suggests that the correct theory, whatever it may be, is not aggregative. Determining the correct view is still an outstanding problem in utilitarian (or—if one prefers—consequentialist) theory.

Honderich says he rejects the (aggregative) utilitarian account of punishment. He has two major reasons for doing so. One is the reason that we have already noted: its counter-intuitive treatment of the one-against-many problem just described (Honderich 2006, 106-107). The other is that utilitarianism allegedly endorses a practice of framing and punishing innocent individuals if that will maximize overall well-being, which seems morally unacceptable.[4] In the next section we will look in detail at this particular objection to utilitarian accounts of punishment, amongst others.

4.2 The basic utilitarian arguments

But first we need to explain how a utilitarian theory can be used to justify state punishment. If the latter is indeed to be defended from a utilitarian standpoint, then it will need to be shown (at the very least) that it has certain consequences that have a positive effect on at least some people's well-being. Some possible ways in which this might be the case will now be listed. (In most cases the ways in which these consequences favor the well-being of at least some people are obvious and will not be explicitly stated.)

1. By incapacitating an offender (e.g. by imprisoning her), we prevent her re-offending.
2. By punishing an offence, we deliver on (and thus make credible) a general threat to punish other offences of the same type, thus reducing the frequency of such offences (deterrence).
3. By legislating that a certain sort of behavior is a punishable offence, we ensure the avoidance of such behavior by those for whom it is habitual to obey the law.
4. By attaching a punishment to a certain sort of behavior, we signal to the population that it is 'seriously wrong,' which discourages this sort of behavior on the part of those members of the population who are appropriately morally motivated. (This is sometimes called the 'educative' function of punishment.)
5. By punishing an offender, we may help to bring about a reform in the offender's character, such that he is less likely to offend in the future.

Consequences 1-5 have in common the feature that they are all expected to lead to some reduction in the frequency of the offences to which they are applied. There are some other consequences, however, that may be thought valuable, although they are not directly linked to crime reduction:

6. Where an offence has an identifiable victim, she (and those close to her) will be made happier (or less unhappy) simply by contemplating the fact that the offender has been 'appropriately' punished. (A variation on this idea is that the whole *community* feels some sort of satisfaction in contemplating the act of punishment.[5])
7. The punishment of an offender may constitute adequate *reparation* to the victim(s).

I want, first of all, to dismiss type (7) consequences as irrelevant to our concern here. This is not because I think that reparation has no legitimate role at all to play in society. It is just that it appears to be governed by different fundamental principles, and so to mix it up with punishment can only cause confusion. In particular, punishment, unlike reparation, is unpleasant by definition, whereas an offender might be able to make adequate reparation to the victim without suffering any distress at all (e.g. if only a moderate sum of money is required and the offender is wealthy). Certainly we cannot expect in general that what is needed for reparation will coincide with what is needed for punishment.

For each of the remaining types of consequences, we need to ask how significant a contribution it is likely to make to the maximization of overall well-being. What we must bear in mind is that punishment normally has bad consequences—indeed, it is expressly designed to create suffering or distress for the person punished. (Also, the threat of punishment may create distress for those whom it causes to abstain from doing what they would like to do.) Whatever good consequences we may expect punishment to have, these must be sufficient to outweigh the bad ones, if punishment is—in utilitarian terms at least—to be morally justifiable.

Bearing this crucial point in mind, I shall next look at two types of consequences that do not appear to pass this test—numbers (5) and (6), which I shall take in reverse order.

When we look at consequences of type (6), concerning the satisfaction that contemplating acts of punishment often gives, we note that justifying punishment in these terms might seem compromised by the fact that the victim is likely to be thinking in retributive terms. But it is not. Simply recognizing the existence of retributive feelings and concerns amongst others (or even in ourselves) and taking these into account in deciding what policies to pursue is not the same as endorsing those feelings or concerns. A utilitarian has to respond to the world as it actually is. That world contains, whether she likes it or not, people who favor retributive justice, enjoying its triumphs and feeling sad at its defeats, quite independently of concerns about crime prevention. The well-being of every person, even the misguided, is equally important to the utilitarian. So we cannot dismiss type (6) consequences as easily as this.

Ted Honderich agrees that 'grievance satisfaction' cannot be excluded as a possible morally relevant consequence of punishment. However, he argues that it is too minor to serve as a *justification* of it: 'Punishment, if that is what justifies it, is not far enough from cutting off someone else's arm in order to improve your sleep' (Honderich 2006, 72). This is surely a little too quick. Some individuals claim to be made very unhappy by the fact that someone who has committed a serious offence against them or someone close to them has received what they consider to be a disproportionately light sentence. In fact, such a person may claim that she has been psychologically devastated by the lenient treatment given to the offender, and that she is therefore suffering something comparable in at least some respects to, say, a life sentence. The critical question is how reliable such victims of crime are when attempting to assess and communicate the effects of such decisions on their own state of mind. If the offender were to receive the level of punishment that the victim would prefer, would the latter really be significantly happier—or significantly less unhappy—as a result? Is it not equally likely that she is very unhappy anyway, because of the long-lasting effects of the original crime, feels enormous anger at the offender, and so comes to believe, without adequate justification, that a more severe punishment would give her peace of mind? To say this is not to belittle the victim's suffering in any way; it is simply to ask a hard question whose answer is supremely relevant here. A harsher punishment for the offender may be what the victim wants; but would it make her less unhappy to an extent sufficient to outweigh the misery of the offender in experiencing that punishment? (Note that retributivism having been rejected, we cannot endorse the idea that the offender *deserves* this misery.)

Unfortunately, this is a question to which, in most cases, it is surely impossible to give any authoritative answer. We have no way of tracing the subtle causal relations involved. Nor can we rely on past experience, as one individual may be quite unlike another in her reactions to events of this kind.

However, I think we can argue the point at a more general level. It strikes me as a dangerous policy to let sentences be determined, even in part, by victims' retributive wishes; the danger would be that of inflating the severity of sentences beyond what is needed for deterrence. Any exceptions to this would be likely to lead to a slippery slope in which retributive feelings eventually take over as the main factor determining sentencing.

We can, I think, dismiss more quickly the other consideration mentioned under type (6) consequences—the feelings of satisfaction that may accrue to members of the community in general as a result of contemplating the punishment of a wicked offender. Again, and for the same reasons as explained above, we cannot dismiss these merely on the grounds that they involve retributive feelings. But we can point to the fact that the difference made to the well-being of those who are not actually victims of the crime or close to the victims is most unlikely to be great enough to outweigh the suffering involved for the offender in the punishment itself.[6]

The second type of consequence which, in my view, is not sufficient to justify punishment is type (5), reform of the offender's character. I should qualify my position here. *If* the attempt to reform offenders through punishment were a generally successful enterprise, then this might be a sufficiently good thing to outweigh the badness of the punishments themselves. But I am skeptical about its success. For one thing, we need to know the answer to a somewhat puzzling question: how *could* hurting someone improve her character? One answer to this question has been offered by R.A. Duff (2001).

Duff maintains that reform is indeed one of the key aims of punishment. The others, he thinks, are *repentance* by the offender and *reconciliation* with the victim of the offence and with the community as a whole—together these constitute the 'three Rs' of punishment. These three aims are closely connected in Duff's theory. Roughly speaking, it seems to be Duff's view that 'repentance' (of a secular kind) leads to both reform and reconciliation.[7] How is this supposed to work? Repentance requires the imposition of hard treatment (as opposed to merely verbal censure or a symbolic punishment), because hard treatment (at least of a certain sort) encourages the offender to reflect deeply about her crime. Duff's thinking here is that true repentance cannot be just momentary, however intense the feelings of guilt (Duff 2001, 108). (As an analogy, he asks us to consider the case of someone who claims to feel grief at the death of a loved one. We would not take this seriously if the person were able to carry on with her life just as normal. Genuine grief must have a deep and long-lasting effect.) If sincere repentance does occur, we can normally expect it to lead to *reform* of the offender's character, whereby she becomes much less likely to offend in the future.

When assessing Duff's account of how he thinks punishment is supposed to operate in order to reform offenders' characters, we need to distinguish clearly between the question of whether things *can* work in the way he describes and the question of whether they typically *do*. Duff does report some success from certain schemes in which offenders are required to engage in 'confrontational group work,' in which they are made to reflect on the consequences of their actions for the victims involved. (For Duff, this counts as 'hard treatment' and therefore qualifies as punishment.) Still, it is difficult to believe that this operation, if practised on a large scale, would have any other effect than to produce, in most cases, merely temporary changes of attitude or, in some instances, totally feigned apologies that would have no lasting effect on the future behavior of the offenders involved. Without larger-scale studies showing the same effect, I am skeptical particularly about the potential of the hard treatment aspect—the *uncomfortableness* of the process—to bring about long-lasting reform.

In doubting the general efficacy of punishment for improving an offender's character, I am not of course questioning the suggestion that offenders can emerge from custody with a reduced tendency to offend. But in most cases it is plausible to think that such an improvement (when it has not been caused by deterrence, which we are not concerned with at this point) has been brought about *in spite of* the punitive aspects of the regime to which they have been subjected, and not because of them. (They may, for example, have benefited from various sorts of educational programmes, or perhaps from certain kinds of therapy which they have been permitted to receive while in jail.)

I shall now examine consequences of types (1) to (4). I begin with type (1): incapacitation. Now that this contributes to crime reduction can hardly be doubted. The most common form of incapacitation for serious crimes (and sometimes, unfortunately, for not so serious ones) is imprisonment. While in prison, an offender will find it very difficult to carry out various sorts of crimes (sometimes impossible, depending on the type of crime involved and the level of control within the prison). This huge reduction in the *ability* of offenders to commit crimes undoubtedly results in many crimes that would otherwise have occurred not in fact occurring. On the other hand, there are other effects of imprisonment that tend to be crime-*conducive*. For example, when the offender is released, she may feel resentful and, as a result, *more* inclined to commit crimes than previously. In addition, offenders sometimes make friendships in jail that have the effect of further entrenching them in a life of crime. One should therefore be cautious when assessing the overall effectiveness of imprisonment as a means of net crime reduction through incapacitation.

The most effective way of incapacitating offenders is to execute them. However, the death penalty carries with it costs that are more dramatic than those attached to imprisonment. There is the offender's horror in knowing that she will die at a certain predictable time (Glover 1977, 233), the difficulty of devising a form of execution that is known to be pain-free and the often devastating effect, emotionally and sometimes materially, on the loved-ones of the offender. When one considers these costs, the use of execution as a method of incapacitation for any offender, even a serious one, begins to look decidedly unattractive. (There is also the danger discussed in the previous chapter concerning the execution of innocent individuals, but in the context of a desert-free theory, assessing the significance of this is not straightforward—see below, Sec. 4.3 under 'Innocent victims.')

Now for deterrence. The first thing we may note is that deterrence does not *necessarily* require anybody to be punished. For the *threat* to punish might, theoretically, result in 100% compliance. In practice, compliance is rarely 100%, but typically much lower. Hence, in assessing the consequentialist value of deterrent punishment, one obviously has to take into account the costs of actually punishing—chief amongst them being (as before) the suffering it causes to the offender.

By threatening to punish, we may be deterring a person from one of two things. The first is the offence itself. The second is the act of committing the offence *openly*, i.e., without attempt at concealment. It may seem as if there would be no value in the latter sort of deterrence, and it is certainly true that the emphasis in most discussions is almost always on the former. How does it help society if offences are being committed in secret instead of openly? To understand how, note that concealment of an offence requires some effort. Therefore, removing the threat of punishment, and hence the necessity of concealment, would make crime generally easier. And, all other things being equal, if the ease with which a certain type of thing can be done is increased and many want to do this type of thing, it will become much more frequent. To take a concrete example: many more burglaries would be committed if they could be done openly without the fear that detection would bring bad consequences for the burglars. But the general point applies to almost every kind of offence.[8] And societies do not survive situations in which almost any kind of offence can be openly committed, for the result is a Hobbesian 'war of all against all.' From now on, when I talk of deterrence, I wish to be understood as including deterrence directed at the *open* committal of crimes. (Of course, in the case of those who doubt that they would be successful in concealing either their crime or the fact that it was they who committed it, the familiar type of deterrence, directed at the act itself, is still important.)

Another useful distinction, and a more standard one, is that between *individual* deterrence and *general* deterrence. The former is involved when a criminal avoids future offending because of her previous experience of punishment and her consequent desire not to be subjected to it again. The latter is when members of the public in general are deterred by the threat of punishment. (Obviously, if successful, this should prevent some people from becoming offenders in the first place.) In popular discussions of punishment the latter form of deterrence tends to be neglected in favor of the former. Thus it is often suggested that high recidivism rates show that prison is useless. This argument, however, only addresses the individual deterrent effect of imprisonment on those who have already experienced it. It overlooks the possibility that many who have never experienced imprisonment may be discouraged from offending by the prospect of it (not to mention non-deterrent effects of prison, such as incapacitation).

An obvious question to ask about deterrent punishment is: does it work? Does it really result in fewer offences? Johs Andenaes gives the example of a blacked-out city in an occupied country. The citizens may not recognize the moral authority of the occupier, but the punitive risks attached to letting the tiniest crack of light show are enough to achieve almost 100% compliance and this is what we find in practice (Andenaes 1971, 145). While it would be absurd to conclude from such cases that deterrent punishment is always effective, they do suggest that it sometimes is. Indeed, it could be argued that *general* deterrence is a much more significant effect of punishment than incapacitation, since it affects a larger group of potential offenders, thus preventing a larger number of offences. In fact, it could be further argued that the presence of even quite a minimal system of deterrent punishment is crucial in preventing a collapse of civilized society—consider what happens in places like post-war Iraq when the forces of law and order break down. If this is right, we can say that because the collapse of society is such a bad thing from a utilitarian point of view, punishment as general deterrence must be considered by utilitarians to be of supreme importance.[9]

Turning now to type (3) consequences, does punishment achieve conformity through habituation? The suggestion is, in other words, that some people obey the law, and thus avoid punishment, simply because it is habitual for them to do so (Andenaes 1971, 142). In such cases they are not actually *deterred*, because they do not consciously think of the possible punitive consequences of offending—habit ensures obedience before such thoughts emerge. While this is unlikely to be true for everyone, it is surely plausible to suppose that it does apply to a significant number of individuals. The habit will originally have come about in any of a range of ways, e.g., moral guidance from others, the person's own moral reflections, or even through fear of punitive consequences—so deterrence may originally have been involved, but no longer once habit has taken over.

Type (4) consequences, pertaining to the 'educative' function of punishment, must also be recognized as playing a role. For many individuals, it is surely the case that making something illegal and attaching to it a significant penalty (such as a term of imprisonment) signals that it is seriously morally wrong, providing an independent reason for desisting from it, quite independently of the fear that may be caused by the deterrent threat (Ewing 1929).

I think that it is very plausible to suggest that consequences of types (1) to (4) are collectively sufficient in their crime-reducing effects to outweigh the bad consequences of punishment—indeed, type (2) (deterrence) may be sufficient on its own for this. Even though there is a cost in terms of misery to those punished, the harm prevented seems vastly more significant than the harm caused, and this seems to be the case particularly when we consider the threat that crime poses to civilized society itself. The latter is not something that can be definitively proven. We simply do not have the mass of information that would be needed to predict the course of events in each of the two possible scenarios (that in which state punishment is retained and that in which it is abandoned) with sufficient accuracy and comprehensiveness—nor could we. A broad-brush assessment is all we are capable of here. Nor do we need it to be certain that these dire consequences would follow the removal of state punishment for the argument to go through. They are *so* dire that their mere likelihood is sufficient.

However, before we can definitely conclude that punishment is justifiable from a utilitarian perspective, there is another line of argument that needs to be considered. This is that the same (or more) benefit can be achieved for less overall cost by 'therapy' rather than punishment. On this model, crime is conceived of as the symptom of an 'illness,' rather than as a sign of moral wickedness. The therapeutic model seems to fit with hard determinism. If a person's tendency to commit offences is strictly beyond her control, as hard determinists maintain, then it does indeed resemble a kind of illness. In that case, discovering the 'cause' of this illness and devising a 'cure' would seem to be the rational response. However, it is both unwise and unnecessary for utilitarians who favor therapy over punishment to appeal to hard determinism; unwise, because hard determinism is not widely accepted (although I did my best to defend it in an earlier chapter); and unnecessary, because the key point for the utilitarian is the overall consequences of a therapeutic regime, as compared with a punitive one. If the former is likely to do better on this score than the latter, then the utilitarian should prefer it for that reason, and that reason alone.

But could a purely therapeutic regime be sufficient to control crime? We could presumably only treat those who are already known to have offended, since it is only to them that we could clearly justify attributing a tendency to commit offences in the future. What about those who have not yet offended? It seems that we still need something like deterrent punishment to keep first offenders to a minimum.

The advocate of therapy might seek to refute this argument by questioning the assumption that we can only justifiably attribute a tendency to commit offences to known offenders. Perhaps, she might suggest, every human being could be monitored from birth (or even *in utero*) to detect signs of potential criminality, and suitable measures (behavioral or pharmacological) taken to prevent this criminal behavior emerging. In this way, it seems that adequate measures *could* be taken to prevent crime from the very beginning, without having to resort to punishment at all.

In advocating such an ambitious plan, the supporters of the therapeutic approach would be making a big assumption, which is that the therapeutic technology they need can actually be developed and made to work successfully. This is far from obviously true. In any case, besides this technical question, there is also an important moral objection, which is that the massive therapeutic regime envisaged would constitute an enormous encroachment on people's civil liberties, especially (but perhaps not only) where it involved the treatment of those who have not yet offended. This encroachment on the freedom of the individual seems to condemn the proposal from the very start. True, a utilitarian could blithely say that she is not interested in civil liberties as such, but only in maximizing well-being. However, I do not wish to disallow the possibility of important moral considerations of a non-utilitarian sort. Nor should it be thought that determinists are unsusceptible to this objection, for they may wish to give due moral weight to civil liberties, understanding them in terms of lack of coercion, rather than in terms of absolute undetermined free will.

However, this last objection seems to be assuming that a therapeutic regime for dealing with crime must be based on compulsion. But although compulsion does have the merit of guaranteeing that the 'patient' will actually be treated, it is not an essential requirement of anti-crime therapy any more than it is for normal medical therapy. Furthermore, most forms of officially recognized psychological therapy—such as cognitive behavior therapy and anger management courses[10]—require the patient's active cooperation. We might insist that all anti-crime therapy should be optional, and justify such a requirement either by reference to individual freedom valued for its own sake, or by arguing that compulsory therapy is for the most part *utilitarianly* wrong,[11] since its practitioners could not always be trusted to use it in a morally acceptable way.

However, I do not think that we could accept a scheme of optional therapy as a complete response to the problem of crime. What if a large number of potential or actual offenders refuse such therapy as we are able to offer, with the result that crime levels remain unacceptably high? Another problem arises irrespective of whether therapy is compulsory or optional: while it is in progress, some offenders may still need to be incapacitated to prevent their re-offending. Thus therapy and punishment should not be seen as mutually incompatible—on the contrary, I believe both should be used together in seeking to maintain a reasonably well-ordered and crime-free society.[12] In fact, in so far as some therapy is already used in most developed countries, such systems are already in place, but of course in any given system of this sort, one can question whether a good balance between punishment and therapy has been achieved.

There is another alternative to punishment worth mentioning besides therapy: 'positive reinforcement.' This concept from behaviorist psychology refers to the practice of attaching rewards to desired behavior (unlike punishment, which attaches penalties to *un*desired behavior). This approach could be applied in relation to the citizenry as a whole. For example, the state could offer a sum of money to anyone who reaches the age of twenty without having offended, with perhaps further rewards at later 'milestones' (e.g. forty years, sixty years). Again, it is unlikely that this could entirely replace the use of punishment. The latter is bound to have a role for three reasons. Firstly, some citizens will simply not have the self-control to stop themselves offending before they can receive the next award that would be due to them. Secondly, some crimes are simply irrational acts, undertaken without concern with either penalty or reward. Thirdly, for any reward that we could conceive, there are some who would conceive of a crime which *for them* would provide a greater reward.

To conclude this part of the discussion, we are now in a position to assert, I think, that state punishment (albeit in combination with various other forms of response) is justified in utilitarian terms. But what of the objection that utilitarianism is the wrong approach anyway—that it fails to take account of some important moral considerations besides the fact that punishment causes suffering? In the next section I shall examine various forms that this objection may take and attempt to answer them.

4.3 Objections to utilitarian punishment and responses

I shall tackle three major objections to the utilitarian theory of punishment. The first states that deterrent punishment in particular does not respect the freedom or autonomy of offenders; the second deals with the objection concerning the theory's treatment of innocent people; and the third states that the theory's consequences in relation to marginalized members of society are unacceptable.

The autonomy objection

Hegel thought that deterrent punishment treated an offender 'like a dog instead of with the freedom and respect due to him as a man' (Hegel 1942, 246). R.A. Duff, whose reformative view of punishment we briefly examined above, quotes this with approval (Duff 2001, 14). In place of such a manipulative conception of punishment, Duff wants us to see punishment as part of a process of rational engagement with the offender, appealing to the latter's understanding of the community's shared values. In other words, it is a matter of persuasion rather than coercion. The aim is not simply that citizens refrain from crime; 'it is, rather, that citizens recognize and accept the law's requirements as being justified and refrain from crime for that reason . . .' (Duff 2001, 81). Thus rational persuasion, as opposed to mere coercion, deception, bullying or manipulation, is the appropriate response to offending behavior. And this is so, Duff maintains, even when we are dealing with hardened criminals who refuse to be persuaded. We owe it to the victim and to the offender himself to make the attempt, even in cases where we know this to be futile (Duff 2001, 82).

We have already raised doubts about the practical effectiveness of Duff's model of punishment. What we are concerned with here, though, is the charge that deterrent punishment disrespects the autonomy of offenders. However, if hard determinism is correct, none of us has true autonomy in the first place, as we are never, literally speaking, in control of what happens to us, even when we are conventionally said to perform 'free' acts. (Duff himself does not consider the determinist argument.) If the behavior of offenders and potential offenders is not controlled by deterrent threats of punishment, then it is controlled by other things. Even in the 'best' case, where an individual's conformity to morality is purely the result of acknowledging a moral truth, the determinist view is that his behavior is simply compelled by that acknowledgement and therefore not 'up to him.' Indeed, Duff himself speaks of 'moral or rational compulsion' in such a case (Duff 2001, 116). The offender is being compelled to accept the truth, in the same sort of way that one can be compelled to accept the evidence of one's senses or to accept the conclusion of a rigorous proof. Duff maintains that the offender is still free to accept or reject the message according to the dictates of his own conscience, and in this sense we have not violated his autonomy. Yet surely to say that the offender has been 'morally or rationally compelled' is straightforwardly incompatible with supposing that he has exercised autonomy.

On the other hand, it is not unreasonable to suppose that that there is something crude about deterrence. It appeals to the selfish part of people's mentality, instead of engaging their moral understanding, as Duff would like us to do. Furthermore, it consists in nothing more than the issuing of threats, which is a technique used by many in actions that deliberately flout morality. Neither of these arguments necessarily presupposes that any person has genuine autonomy, and so they do not follow the letter of Duff's objection, but they do seem to be in the spirit of it.

However, the fact that a certain type of action is used by many to flout morality is not in itself a reason to reject it for our own use. The purpose of state punishment is to make life more bearable for all or at least most of us, and this has every appearance of being a moral aim—it is not the aim of someone who works *against* morality. And if we *could* achieve this aim solely by engaging people's moral understanding, we would. Indeed, the 'educative' role of punishment has already been recognized as having some contribution to make. However, in addition to those who have a strong sense of right and wrong and use the law partly as a guide to making the distinction in particular cases (and those who have simply grown used to obeying the law), there appear to be a substantial number for whom only deterrence is likely to be effective. If they are not deterred in sufficient numbers, a disastrous situation threatens. So even if we accept that deterrence is crude, and not something we would like to engage in if we could avoid it, the circumstances we are faced with appear to leave us with no feasible alternative.

One last point. Most offenders will need to be compelled by those who administer the system to subject themselves to the process of moral persuasion, and it seems that this can only be achieved by a process of deterrence. Duff himself mentions that imprisonment is available as a last resort, when offenders wilfully refuse to obey the terms of other, more lenient, sentences (Duff 2001, 152). (These more lenient sentences would include the sort of group work scenarios that provide perhaps the best vehicle for moral persuasion.) Now in practice, the sanction of imprisonment might not actually have to be inflicted very often. But this does not alter the fact that many, if not most, offenders will only cooperate with the more lenient procedures because they are at least vaguely aware that failure to do so is likely to result in something worse for them. This is deterrence, pure and simple. Duff is in fact aware that a state punishment system designed along his lines may result in some being deterred from crime because they fear the unpleasantness of the punishments imposed. But he thinks that this is not a problem for him, since the system is not actually *aiming* at deterrence (Duff 2001, 124). However, as we have just seen, deterrence *is* an essential aim of a certain part of his system which ensures that as many offenders as possible undergo the more productive forms of treatment. Hence this *tu quoque* point against Duff is a sound one.

Innocent victims

The second objection to the utilitarian justification of punishment that I need to consider is based on the observation that some of those punished within actual criminal justice systems are innocent of the crimes of which they have been convicted, and this is almost certain to be true even in the most highly developed and conscientiously run systems. For the balance of evidence will in some cases 'objectively' favor the judgment that A is guilty of a crime even though, factually, she is not. And of course if, as is far more often the case, the system is not the most highly developed or not conscientiously run, we can expect there to be even more miscarriages of justice. The accusation is that utilitarians do not take this fact seriously, because of their lack of concern with desert *per se*. Indeed, there is a more developed argument lurking here, which seems even more damaging to the utilitarian case. This is that utilitarians would have no good moral reason to shun a systematic policy of *telishment*,[13] that is, of 'punishing' innocent people, a practice which, while saving the bother of actually investigating crimes, might nevertheless be adequate in deterrent terms.

A hard determinist such as myself might simply say that the problem is illusory, since no-one ever deserves unpleasant treatment anyway, but that unfortunately this is sometimes necessary if crime is to be controlled. However, this response is rather crude, as hard determinism is definitely a minority position, and (as earlier remarked) even I am not totally certain of its truth! It would be much more satisfactory to show that utilitarianism does not in fact have the alleged implication.

Actually, it is not difficult to see that a policy of telishment would probably *not* maintain adequate deterrence. For if such a policy were to be vigorously pursued, it would quickly become known that whether or not a citizen suffered at the hands of the authorities was largely unrelated to whether or not she had done anything wrong, and so the deterrent effect would disappear. Thus the contention that such a policy would maximize well-being seems groundless.

However, there are two ways of recasting the objection so that it still seems threatening to the utilitarian. One is to argue that, although a deliberate and systematic *policy* of telishment might indeed fail to maximize well-being, the same might not apply to a practice of simply letting telishment happen by permitting the lax application of standards of judicial process. For in that case, according to this argument, the *majority* of those punished would probably be guilty, and so adequate deterrence would be maintained, while it would also be true that a great deal of time and expense would be saved because of the absence of any need to apply judicial standards in a thorough and conscientious way. And yet, the argument proceeds, it is clearly wrong to tolerate lax judicial standards and the miscarriages of justice that they would result in, and so this implication of utilitarianism shows the latter to have unacceptable consequences.

This is a harder version of the argument for the utilitarian to repel effectively, because of its claim that a certain form of telishment-based practice would yield adequate deterrence, with the result that the utilitarian's own standards would seem to compel her to accept it. Harder, but not impossible The scenario depicted is not a very stable one. There is some significant risk that the laxness will increase in a 'slippery slope' manner, producing a situation in which the judicial authorities are happy to arrest almost anyone and lock them up with scarcely anything approaching a fair trial. Once this happens, the general citizenry have as much to fear from the police as they have from conventional criminals. It must be considered very important, from a utilitarian point of view, to stay well clear of such a situation. That means avoiding practices which, although they may seem economical in utilitarian terms, risk leading to this sort of eventuality.

The other form that the recast argument could take involves focusing on the alleged utilitarian justifiability of *one-off* cases of telishment. (This has tended to be more popular with anti-utilitarians in any case.) It may be conceded that telishment is wrong as a general practice, whether by default or as the result of a deliberate policy. But in the particular case of a very heinous and very frequent sort of crime, when an example has got to be made of someone and the police cannot find any of the real perpetrators, why shouldn't they simply frame an innocent individual? What is there in utilitarianism that would ground a moral condemnation of this?

I think the problem with this as an argument against the utilitarian view of punishment is that it assumes that, in the circumstances depicted, telishment would be intuitively wrong and this is questionable. I do not claim that, intuitively, telishment *would* be morally acceptable in these circumstances. But I do think it is at least a 'hard case.' For the suggestion that in the circumstances depicted, telishment would indeed produce greater well-being than any possible alternative is far from implausible. The crime is very heinous, which suggests that failure to control it would cause much suffering. If the unfortunate individual is telished, this might create enough deterrent effect to reduce significantly the frequency of the crime, with the consequence that this suffering would be prevented. This deterrent effect could be achieved by punishing the real perpetrators, but that is not possible. In these circumstances it is, I contend, at least defensible to suppose that it would be wrong *not* to telish, that telishing in the way described would be the only morally correct course of action, despite its highly repellent aspect. Roughly speaking, the ultimate reason for this is that it is defensible to suppose that the extreme suffering of the many counts for more than the extreme suffering of just one individual. (Note that this does not involve a commitment to the implausible aggregative theory: we do not suppose that the *minor discomfort* of the many can morally outweigh the suffering of the one.) If I am right, it is not so much a matter of utilitarianism clashing with intuition as of utilitarianism agreeing with one side in a case of conflicting intuitions. I grant that there may be other theories that back the other side. But I have not seen a theory that is so convincing that it removes the sense of conflict, so the utilitarian view is not to be dismissed for failing to do so. In addition, utilitarianism proposes a goal—the maximization of well-being—that has positive intuitive support in a wide range of cases, and is arguably a moral version of ordinary, practical means-ends reasoning. It is thus mistaken, I think, to suppose that the telishment argument succeeds in undermining it.

A summary of my position is as follows. Telishment as a deliberate systematic policy could not be justified in utilitarian terms, contrary to the objection stated, because it would not provide adequate deterrence. Telishment 'by default,' i.e., through the lax application of judicial standards would at least *threaten* to bring about a situation in which citizens had more to fear from the judicial authorities than from conventional criminals, and is therefore also unjustifiable in utilitarian terms. Finally, regarding one-off telishment, while it seems correct to suppose that this *would* be justifiable in utilitarian terms in the type of situation envisaged, it is also plausible to think that this does not clearly constitute a valid objection to utilitarianism, since it may well be that it *is* justifiable in that type of situation for precisely the reason that the utilitarian gives. Nothing better can be said of any other theory in this context.

Consequences for the 'marginalized'

When considering the justifiability of punishment, R.A. Duff cites the example of a severely impoverished single mother stealing clothes from a supermarket for her children. Such a person, he suggests, is excluded from the benefits that are attached to membership of a political community. Is it correct therefore to regard her as being bound by its laws? This question seems to be based on moral notions about the relationship between the individual and the community with which utilitarianism does not directly concern itself.[14] Still, it might be considered a strength for the theory if its prescriptions on this matter did not conflict with the quasi-contractarian intuitions which the question reveals.

The implication of the objection is that for a social arrangement to justifiably demand conformity from all citizens, it is not enough that it should increase overall well-being. It must be the case that for each individual member of the community, it either makes no difference to her level of well-being or it improves it. (It is 'Pareto optimal' in the jargon of welfare economics.) Now it seems that almost every member of society is disadvantaged in one way by membership of a community which employs a criminal justice system—she is restrained from doing some things which she would like to do and, in all likelihood, she has to contribute financially to the cost of maintaining the system that enforces this. In the worst case, she herself will break one or more of the laws and suffer punishment as a result. Therefore, if a criminal justice system is to benefit *everyone*, it must be the case that each person receives sufficient benefit from it to outweigh these drawbacks. This may seem far-fetched, especially in view of Duff's examples. But it is not as obviously false as it appears at first sight. Even the shoplifting single mother benefits from not living in a society characterized by the sort of violence and insecurity that ours would arguably contain if it were not for the deterrent effect (and to a lesser extent) the other crime-reducing effects of state punishment. On the other hand, while it may indeed be the case that she benefits from the existence of *some* state punishment system, as opposed to there being none at all, might it not be best for her if the system were designed in such a way that very poor people were exempted from punishment for certain otherwise criminal actions that would be likely to make their lives more bearable? Perhaps so. However, we obviously need to consider the broader consequences of such a policy. As this is best done when we have before us a fairly detailed theory of utilitarian punishment, I shall postpone this task until the next chapter.[15]

4.4 A return to desert?

At this point, it should be conceded that rather than reject desert as I have done, most utilitarians try to explain and legitimize the concept by making the case that its recognition and application furthers desirable social goals. Haven't I therefore been precipitate in seeking to jettison desert altogether? Shouldn't it rather be *absorbed into* a utilitarian system? There are broadly two ways of doing this, a moderate way and a radical way.

The moderate way accepts that utilitarian considerations must be paramount in both the justification and the design of a penal system, but requires that such considerations be entirely left out of account by judges and others who are involved in administering the system on a day-to-day basis. Instead the latter should be thinking only in terms of desert and its related notions of guilt and innocence (Rawls 1955, 147). The reason for this is at least partly to do with a theoretical distinction between two kinds of utilitarianism: *act utilitarianism* and *rule utilitarianism*.

For an act utilitarian, the morally right act is the one which, in the current circumstances, has the best expected consequences. Act utilitarians have to deal with each individual case on its own merits. This is not without its problems. It places a tremendous burden of deliberation on the agent, and the calculation of expected consequences can often be affected by error or personal bias. For these reasons (and others), some utilitarian philosophers have devised a theory known as 'rule utilitarianism,' which drastically reduces the range of occasions when agents must engage in the direct calculation of expected consequences. According to this view, such purely utilitarian thinking is almost entirely confined to the problem of devising rules or practices which are intended to serve many agents over an extended period of time. For the rule utilitarian, the right act is not necessarily the act with the best expected consequences, but (roughly speaking) the act which is required by a system of rules or practices with the following property: that best consequences would be produced by general conformity to it within society as a whole.

When applied to the punishment of criminals, this approach leaves the utilitarian thinking to those who are responsible for designing a legal system, principally the government. It is they who—theoretically at least—have the time and breadth of view to choose institutions and practices that will maximize overall well-being. Police, judges, jurors and others involved in the actual day-to-day running of the penal system are spared this burden, and those who are tempted towards shouldering any part of it are required to resist that temptation. Their job is simply to follow the rules laid down within the practices themselves.

If one *is* a utilitarian, an approach of this general sort seems unavoidable, whatever the precise details of the penal system involved. The latter cannot simply consist of the single principle, 'maximize expected overall well-being' (the principle of utility), for it would be far too difficult for the officials of the system to apply this on a day-by-day basis—there are too many different possible consequences affecting too many different people, and there is too great a risk of error or bias. That is why we are bound to need rules of procedural justice for making the particular decisions that the officials of the system are called upon to make.[16] Thus the design of the penal system, though it should be based on the utilitarian goal of maximizing well-being, issues in rules that do not explicitly aim at that goal. But an important question arises here: would it be right to say that in applying these rules one would, unlike the designers of the system, be thinking in terms of deservingness, of guilt and innocence?

In a purely formal sense, perhaps so. The person who has been found to have performed the act (with *mens rea*) has been 'found guilty' of the crime; another in whose case there is deemed to be insufficient evidence has been 'found not guilty.' But is it necessarily the case that the person found guilty *deserves* the punishment he is then prescribed? It can happen that, even if the rules of the system are scrupulously applied, a 'blameless' mistake has been made, and she did not actually commit the crime. In such a case it could hardly be claimed that she got what she deserved. (The same point could be made about a person incorrectly acquitted—see Sher 1987, 16.) Nevertheless, it could be argued that the *aim* of the officials applying the rules is that only deserving people should be convicted and punished, and this being so, there does seem to be a role for the concept of desert.

However, if, as was argued in my second chapter, hard determinism is correct, then no-one ever deserves punishment for anything that they do. And in Chapter One it was shown that even if we accept that some people do deserve the punishments they receive, it is all too often impossible to establish this in particular cases. Satisfaction of the rules of a penal system, though it may be taken as showing that *relative to the system*, the prescribed punishment is justified (which is important if the system is a morally good one), does not show that the offender was genuinely responsible for her act, or that her retributive balance would be improved by punishing her, and hence does not demonstrate that she deserves punishment. Thus the moderate way of recovering desert does not even begin to come to grips with the chief arguments against the use of this concept. What about the radical approach?

This approach exemplifies what George Sher calls *institutional* desert.[17] The idea is that the concept of desert gets its very meaning and content from the (utilitarianly designed) ideal practices and institutions of a society. I do not know of any philosopher who has explicitly advocated such a view, but it seems worthy of discussion. Furthermore, as Sher points out, John Rawls adopts a parallel position in which the claims of justice are logically prior to those of desert in the distribution of economic goods and other benefits, though, as it happens, Rawls does not think that justice is determined in a utilitarian way. Here is a paragraph in which he defends his view:

> [T]he concept of moral worth is secondary to those of right and justice, and it plays no role in the substantive definition of distributive shares. The case is analogous to the relation between the substantive rules of property and the law of robbery and theft. These offences and the demerits they entail presuppose the institution of property which is established for prior and independent social ends. For a society to organize itself with the aim of rewarding moral desert as a first principle would be like having the institution of property in order to punish thieves. (Rawls 1971, 313, quoted in Sher 1987, 14.)

Clearly, such a view resembles what I have called the 'radical' view of the relationship between utilitarianism and the concept of desert as it applies to those found guilty of crimes. (The two differences are that the principle of utility has been replaced by a different sort of ethical principle, and the type of deservingness involved relates to distributive justice,[18] rather than to crime and punishment.) Also, one can imagine a defender of the radical utilitarian view using Rawls' analogy with property and the law of theft in support of her own position.

What exactly is radical about the 'radical' position? According to the moderate view, the everyday application of the rules of the penal system reflects our pre-theoretical intuitions about desert, even if the latter are not what ultimately determine those rules. An official of the system is able and expected to make decisions in ways that largely accord with those intuitions. On the radical view, in contrast, the official, while he may be applying *a* concept of desert, is not applying the familiar concept that we all know, but rather a revised one, tailored to fit the utilitarian principle. Whereas the familiar concept of desert is incompatible with determinism (or so I have claimed), the revised concept is not. There is no attempt at trickery here. We know very well that we cannot alter logical relationships between propositions by linguistic sleight of hand. What happens is merely that we now use a certain word—'desert'—to refer to something different from what it previously denoted.

Why might we want to do this? Well, this word has long existed in our language and has a specific sort of role. It makes sense to try to retain the word, because of its familiarity and this well understood role. It serves to refer, broadly speaking, to appropriate ways of treating people on the basis of their actions or qualities. However, this aspect does not constitute the totality of the word's meaning. Also contained in this is the link between desert and the concepts of free will and moral responsibility, which explains the incompatibility between determinism and desert. This element of meaning is eliminated on the radical strategy. It is eliminated because, being a determinist, but at the same time finding good (utilitarian) reason to punish, the radical theorist wants to carry on saying that those punished should be those who *deserve* to be punished, despite their failing to satisfy conventional criteria of moral responsibility.

All this seems fine in principle. The problem is one of practicality. Philosophers *have* occasionally suggested that words be changed to suit a goal which, through their theorizing, they conceive to be worth pursuing. But frankly, they do not have much power in these matters. Ordinary language will evolve as it does, and philosophers have very little influence over it. Of course, one could adopt the more modest aim of trying to get *other philosophers* to adopt one's preferred usage. But while this might work for technical terms, it is unlikely to be successful with parts of everyday vocabulary such as 'desert.'

So neither the moderate nor the radical view of how to re-instate desert within a theoretical framework that is both utilitarian and determinist appear convincing. I think it is time for us to conclude that no such thing is possible, and that the concept of desert should be banished from the theory of punishment.

Notes

1. For an accessible and combative account of the issues, including punishment, see Smart and Williams 1973.

2. This is a simplified account. In a full treatment one would have to deal with the fact that, for example, each individual enjoys different levels of well-being at different times.

3. Honderich is inclined to think that any sensible moral philosophy must be consequentialist, but this (as he realizes) is controversial (Honderich 2006, 235).

4. Honderich 2006, 89-104. Both this and the aggregative utilitarian's decision in favor of the many in the one-against-many scenario specified above are described by him as cases of 'victimization.' Actually, in order to show that the

former would be endorsed by aggregative utilitarianism (which Honderich rejects), but not by consequentialism (which he accepts), it would obviously be necessary to show that it is specifically the *aggregative* method that has this consequence, and it is far from obvious that this can be done.

5. This is somewhat reminiscent of Joel Feinberg's 'expressive' theory of punishment, though Feinberg does not advocate his view from a specifically utilitarian perspective. (See Feinberg 1970, 95-118.)

6. *Aggregative* utilitarians might dispute this. They might suggest that the small increases in well-being experienced by the mass of ordinary citizens in feeling or expressing abhorrence could *collectively* outweigh the intense suffering of the relatively small number who undergo severe punishment. But we have already commented on how counter-intuitive the aggregative theory is, and precisely because of this sort of implication.

7. Duff does not regard himself as a consequentialist. A consequentialist will approve of *any* means to achieve the good consequences of punishment that do not involve sufficiently serious counterbalancing costs. Duff's view is more restrictive, involving the idea that the end itself dictates what means are acceptable. That end is reconciliation through reform and repentance. (See Duff 2001, 98.)

8. In this context 'concealment of an offence' means concealment of it while it is occurring, the ultimate aim being of course concealment of the perpetrator's identity.

9. We can therefore reasonably suggest that any system of law and order—even a somewhat unjust one—is better than none at all. In Chapter Eight of his book on punishment Honderich almost appears to imply otherwise (Honderich 2006, 195-227). Of course, a just system is better than both of these situations.

10. Not forgetting vitally important programs to help people come off alcohol and other drugs.

11. Compulsion might be used in the rare case of a highly dangerous individual for whom the relevant therapy would be a cost-effective course of action.

12. The anti-therapy position may have been influenced, not only by high-minded arguments about human dignity, but also by the assumption that a therapeutic system will treat people in a way that everyone would agree to be unacceptable. Here one should note the influence of the anti-psychiatry movement,

which seems to have come at a time in the sixties when such extreme measures as ECT and lobotomies were overused treatments. (It is harder to object to such essentially benign measures as cognitive behavior therapy.) The novel and film of *A Clockwork Orange* seem typical of the ethos of the time.

13. A term coined by John Rawls. Rawls' concept was actually a little more specific than this, imposing somewhat tighter constraints on the officials administering the system (Rawls 1955, 151-2).

14. Indeed, Duff himself does not raise them specifically as anti-utilitarian points, but more as difficulties for an approach like his own, which stresses the idea of belonging to a community and sees punishment as a response to the violation of the laws of that community. His own solution is to suggest that as long as social injustices of this kind continue, punishment will always be morally tainted, but that it is partially justified if we, as a community, are conscientiously working to eliminate social injustice (Duff 2001, 199).

15. See the discussion of Alison's case below, Sec. 5.5.

16. However, it does not necessarily follow that act utilitarianism must be abandoned. If the point of the rules is merely to provide answers to the question of what (in the sort of case to which each is applicable) would maximize expected overall well-being, then it seems that the principle of utility is after all the ultimate grounding of whatever actions the rules require, even though that may not be obvious from the standpoint of the officials involved. But this is a complex matter. Some utilitarian writers think that rules other than the principle of utility itself have exactly this sort of superficial role. Others think that some such rules could not be dispensed with even in principle. There is no consensus. Fortunately, the issue is not of paramount importance to us here.

17. See Sher 1987, 12-17. Actually Sher runs together the moderate and radical views under this heading, whereas I prefer to distinguish them.

18. For a discussion of Rawls' ideas governing distributive justice, see below, Sec. 6.2.

CHAPTER FIVE
UTILITARIAN PUNISHMENT IN DETAIL

5.1   Guiding Principles

We have now answered the main objections raised against the utilitarian approach to punishment. It is now time to investigate how the theory might be developed in some detail. In particular, we need to determine the answer to a large, but quite specific question: how should we go about deciding what is the correct sentence to impose on an offender for each given type and severity of offence?

The great classical utilitarian, Jeremy Bentham proposed a number of rules intended to be applied by judges in determining 'the right sentence.' One of these is:

> The greater the mischief of the offence, the greater is the expense, which it may
> be worth while to be at, in the way of punishment. (Bentham 1988, 181)

This entails a principle of proportional punishment, as can be seen by the illustration that Bentham provides for it: if burning alive is ever a permissible punishment, it is more so for murder or arson than it is for, say, the making of counterfeit money. The utilitarian justification of this principle is not hard to discern. It is a simple matter of weighing cost and benefit. There is more benefit in punishing a more serious offence than a less serious one, since there is more benefit in reducing the frequency of a serious crime than in reducing the frequency of a less serious one. So a greater cost can be tolerated for the former than for the latter. Chiefly, the greater cost consists in the greater degree to which the punishment is unpleasant or painful. Clearly, there is no point increasing the cost of a punishment unless some extra and overriding benefit emerges *from that extra cost*. This extra benefit of punishing must be *due* to the extra cost—or more precisely to whatever generates it. Assuming deterrence to be effective at all (and we defended that claim in the previous chapter), this demand seems to be satisfied when the extra cost lies in increased unpleasantness. By threatening a more unpleasant punishment (and therefore having to deliver on this threat when the relevant sorts of wrongdoings are committed), we increase the deterrent effect—and we need that increased deterrent effect most of all in the case of the most serious offences—i.e., those whose decreased frequency will provide the most benefit. So the significance of deterrence is implicit in the operation of Bentham's principle quoted above. And indeed, this provides a clear answer to those retributivists who think that only *their* theory can convincingly ground proportionality in punishment.

But there is a problem. I asserted above that by threatening more unpleasant punishments, we increase the deterrent effect. However, this may not always be true, and when it is true, the amount of increased deterrence may not always be sufficient to justify the suffering involved. There may be an upper limit beyond which any increase in unpleasantness would not seem practically significant to anyone threatened with it. (Nobody, for example, would be more deterred by the prospect of ten years and one week of torture than by the prospect of just ten years of torture.) Also, the number of offenders who would need a very draconian punishment to deter them (as opposed to something lighter) may be only a small minority, in which case the extra deterrent effect might not be large enough to justify the cost in suffering.

This is a question to which empirical research seems highly relevant. However, drawing firm conclusions is often difficult. A particular jurisdiction might increase the severity of the sentence attached to a particular type of offence, and this may be followed by a fall in the frequency of that type of offence, but how can one be sure that the fall was due to the crack-down or caused by other factors entirely? (Of course, a similar drop reported from different studies in different places and suggesting the same conclusion may provide a little more confidence.)

None of this throws doubt on the proportionality principle *per se*. It shows only that it is difficult to apply in practice. However, even the *theory* of proportionality may be more complex than we have suspected. What I am calling *the* Principle of Proportionality may be stated as follows.

Principle of Proportionality:
The severity of a punishment should be directly proportional to the gravity of the offence.

But Bentham draws attention to some other proportionality principles. Some of these are rather minor, but there is one that appears to be more important. He states it thus:

> The value of the punishment must not be less in any case than what is sufficient to outweigh that of the profit of the offence. (Bentham 1988, 179)

'Profit' does not necessarily mean monetary gain here—it is the anticipated degree of pleasure or well-being. His point is that this factor determines the strength of the temptation, and if the punishment is not sufficiently severe to outweigh this, then it will be useless.[1]

One question that we might pose about this principle is whether it is intended for individual deterrence, general deterrence, or both. At first sight, it seems that individual deterrence makes the most sense here, for it is sometimes possible to know, of a particular individual, roughly how much she will be tempted towards a given course of action, whereas one cannot know this about a large number of anonymous citizens. But there is a problem with this, in that criminal laws and the sentences attached to their violation are not announced to particular individuals, but to the citizenry as a whole. So to make practical sense in the context of judicial punishment, it seems that Bentham must actually be talking about general deterrence. And there are indeed two ways in which a principle of this sort might be thought to serve general deterrence. The first is that when a person is considering whether to perform a particular type of act, she may be affected by the knowledge that acts of this type are normally punished with such-and-such a degree of severity. That amount of severity should have been correctly calculated (though she need not know this) as being what is sufficient to outweigh the amount of temptation to which those contemplating performing such an act are normally subjected. Consequently, she will desist from performing it. But the trouble with this is that one cannot in fact associate types of act with degrees of temptation in this way. The type of act that we call 'robbing a large bank' may constitute a big temptation to some, but only a minimal temptation to others. But there is a second possibility. Perhaps penalties will be attached to degrees of temptation rather than to types of offences, and the potential offender is aware of how much temptation she is feeling, and furthermore knows that this amount of temptation meets with such-and-such a degree of severity from the criminal law, enough to outweigh it. But this is surely attributing an unrealistically subtle level of knowledge to the potential offender. It would rarely obtain in practice. For these reasons, I do not think that we should set too much store by this alternative proportionality principle of Bentham's. In my view, the one that I have described as *the* Principle of Proportionality seems sufficient. If I am right, we should be relieved, since it is easy to see that if it were necessary to operate both principles, conflicts would sometimes result, as they determine the severity of sentences in entirely different ways.

Having spent some time discussing the matter from a philosopher's point of view, I now want to adopt a very different perspective: that of a judge deciding on the correct sentence for an offender—or alternatively, a parole board member considering whether a prison inmate is 'fit for release into the community.' One way in which this perspective differs greatly from that so far adopted is the fact that those occupying it do not usually say much about general deterrence (though they may sometimes allude to it, as when a judge says that to give a light sentence in a particular case would be 'to send the wrong signal'). Mostly they tend to be concerned with other things. One such thing is desert, but I maintain of course that this is a misguided concern. Another is individual deterrence. A third is reform, either by means of the punishment itself or (more plausibly) by means of activities undertaken while in custody. As far as parole boards are concerned, the key question is whether the individual is any longer a 'danger to society.' Have there been effects, related either to individual deterrence or to character reform, sufficient to produce a change in the offender, such that the chance of his re-offending if released is zero or tolerably small? Implicit in the concentration on this issue is the role of imprisonment as an incapacitating measure. While he is in prison, members of the public are 'safe' from the offender, as he is simply unable to carry out any crimes against them. Out of prison, he would again have that ability, and so before releasing him, it is considered vital to know whether he would be significantly inclined to do so.

This approach is fraught with difficulties of an epistemic nature. It is notoriously hard to know whether individual offenders are still significantly disposed towards crime after release, and some terrible mistakes have been made. On the other hand, it might be argued that it is unrealistic to expect one hundred per cent success, and the occasional disasters, while indeed tragic, do not in themselves entail that the system as a whole is ripe for major reform. But is a system of this kind likely to produce consistency and inspire confidence in the operation of criminal justice? Parole boards struggle to assess the implications of different items of information, with one member placing emphasis on a factor that seems relatively unimportant to another. It is not that they are necessarily biased by their philosophical or political views. Even when lacking such crude partiality, their decisions can be highly subjective, i.e., such that an equally reasonable person might take the opposite view. And as far as the original sentencing is concerned, judges as a group do not appear to show much consistency, some being tough, others lenient. Maximum or minimum sentences set by statute help a little. But these laws always leave a significant area of discretion, intended to enable the judge to vary the sentence according to the peculiarities of the case, and this is where the scope for variation between different judges arises.

What is needed, in my view, is a set of very simple rules, together with minimal use of judicial discretion. Such an approach would be hard for judges to get used to, but once entrenched in their practice, it would result in much greater judicial consistency and probably, as a result of this, greater confidence in the criminal justice system.

But before we get into the details of such a system, there is an important contrast to be drawn between the deterrent and incapacitating roles of punishment. This is the fact that the most extreme forms of incapacitation (the death penalty and life imprisonment), unlike the most severe forms of deterrent punishment, have a strong element of certainty associated with them. If an offender's life is taken by the state, then it is certain that she will not offend again. Also, if an offender is subjected to lifetime confinement, she will not offend against the general public again, and offences against those who look after her can be made very difficult by the conditions of her confinement. Nothing comparable applies to extreme forms of punishment intended primarily as a deterrent. The actual effects, in terms of individual and general deterrence, of the most unpleasant and extreme punishments are a matter of speculation. (Empirical evidence may help, but is rarely decisive.) The implication that I want to draw from this is that there is more reason to adopt extreme forms of treatment when the aim is incapacitation than when it is deterrence, simply because we have a greater guarantee of benefit in the former case. I have in mind particularly the example of a serial killer who has already murdered several times. Such a person is very likely to kill again if left at large within the community. There will therefore be a great gain in net expected (general) well-being if such a person is either executed or sentenced to life imprisonment. To impose the same sentence for purely deterrent reasons would be much riskier in terms of its cost-benefit implications—indeed, it is for this reason that I reject extreme forms of punishment, such as execution, life imprisonment and torture, as methods of deterrence.

Because of this specific cost-benefit difference between incapacitation and deterrence, I think we need two distinct systems: one governing the treatment of very dangerous offenders and aimed at total incapacitation (but with some welcome deterrent effect in addition, no doubt), and the other aimed at the rest, whose objective is primarily deterrence (but with a welcome side-effect of temporary incapacitation if imprisonment is used).

In principle at least, the first system will be relatively straightforward. One simply has to ask whether the offender, if released back into the community is extremely likely to re-offend in a very serious (e.g. life-threatening) manner. In view of some of my earlier comments, this may not *sound* straightforward. However, the key lies in the words 'extremely likely.' In general, if the offender has already seriously offended *twice*, and there is no great reason to think that this was a fluke, or that there has been any relevant change of character on her part, then she may be regarded as 'extremely likely' to seriously re-offend and thus a good candidate for indefinite incapacitation.[2]

What form should the incapacitation take? Rather than lay down either option of execution or life imprisonment for every case, I believe that the most humane way of achieving permanent incapacitation is to follow a suggestion once made in discussion by A.J. Ayer, which involves offering the offender a choice between state-assisted suicide and lifetime confinement (or at least confinement until old age has rendered him incapable of harming anyone). I should again emphasize that this course is not recommended for offenders of whom it cannot be said that they are 'extremely likely' to re-offend, for example, one-off murderers. Such murderers, by definition, are not likely to kill again, and therefore do not require this extreme treatment.

I turn now to the second, deterrent-based, system. For this I have a proposal that takes the form of an algorithm for determining sentences which, I suggest, could be learned quite quickly by a group of intelligent people (say, in half a day), and such that there would be a high extent of agreement in the results that they get from it, given the same basic information to start with (higher, I would claim, than with a conventional system). I do not claim, by the way, that it is the *only* feasible system that could be used for good sentencing, just that it is *a* feasible system. After presenting the algorithm, I demonstrate its hypothetical use in three real-life cases.

5.2 The S-score algorithm

The S-score algorithm determines a value, called the *S-score* ('sentencing score'), for each *sentencing episode*, i.e., each occasion when sentencing is required. An S-score is determined in such a way as to represent the overall severity of the sentence, with a higher S-score representing a more severe sentence. In addition to the S-score algorithm, a method is needed for mapping S-scores onto actual sentences e.g. numbers of years in prison. But our first task is to state the S-score algorithm itself. To speak roughly, an S-score is found by adding together a set of *C-scores* (component scores), each of which corresponds to a single type of offence which is under consideration in a given sentencing episode.[3] The first part of the S-score algorithm is the C-score algorithm, which determines the C-score for a given type of offence.

Most of the clauses of the C-score algorithm (given below) are reasonably self-explanatory, but C1 and C3 need some prior explanation. C1 appeals to the distinction between *mala in se* and *mala prohibita*. A *malum in se* (literally, an 'evil in itself') is a type of act which is disallowed by the criminal law because it is morally wrong. A *malum prohibitum* (a 'prohibited evil') is a type of act which is disallowed by the criminal law, not because it is morally wrong, but simply because *some* regulation is needed, and this prohibition has come to fulfil this role for more-or-less arbitrary reasons. An example would be driving on the left-hand side of the road in a country where right-hand driving is legally required—driving on the left in such circumstances is not immoral, or at least, if it is, that is not why it is legally disallowed.[4] It is legally disallowed simply because *some* regulation of this kind is needed to prevent chaos on the roads. (Having everyone drive on the left is of course a perfectly valid alternative.)

However, I should explain that I believe the concept of a *malum prohibitum* to have a wider application than is traditionally supposed. I believe that theft, for example, is a *malum prohibitum*, rather than a *malum in se*. Some acts of theft—such as those where the victim is a billionaire and the amount stolen is paltry—are arguably not immoral in themselves. The only reason that we might have for regarding them as immoral is that theft is illegal and it is immoral to break the law. Even those who do regard all theft as immoral independently of the law (for example, Christians who believe that the Ten Commandments are the authentic word of God) might agree that this is not the reason that theft is contrary to *secular* law. We have laws against theft because access and control over goods have to be regulated in some way (for utilitarian reasons, I would suggest), and nobody has been able to devise or enforce a better way of doing this than by means of the sorts of laws against theft that we have. This point about the wide application of the concept of a *malum prohibitum* should be borne in mind when considering the implications of the S-score algorithm.

As far as *mala in se* are concerned, the algorithm accords with utilitarian thinking in seeing the immorality involved as relating to anticipated harm to others.[5] Consequently, C3 uses the concept of a *harm-making property* possessed by a type of act. An example of a harm-making property would be the certainty of causing long-term, but not disastrous, harm to a limited number of people. Another example of such a property would be the likelihood of causing disastrous harm for many people. As the examples illustrate, possible harm-making properties can be constructed by varying three parameters: (a) level of harm (short-term, long-term non-disastrous, long-term disastrous); (b) number of people affected (a limited number or many) and probability (certain or merely likely).

I now present the C-score algorithm.

C-score algorithm:

(C1) If this type of offence is a *malum prohibitum* and does not satisfy C2 or C3 below, set the C-score to 1.

(C2) If this type of offence is a *malum prohibitum and* is likely or certain to result in only short-term harm (i.e. significant but temporary distress or pain) for one or more individuals, set the C-score to 2.

(C3) If this type of offence is likely to cause long-term harm to one or more people, calculate the C-score by the following procedure:

  (a) For each harm-making property of this type of offence:

  Calculate the product *hnp*, using the following rules to determine the values of h, n and p:

  If it is long-term, but not disastrous,[6] harm, $h = 4$.
  If it is disastrous, long-term harm, $h = 8$.

  If the harm would affect a limited number of people, $n = 1$.
  If the harm would affect a large number of people, $n = 2$.

  If, given that the offence is committed, the harm is only likely, as opposed to certain or near-certain, to occur, $p = 1$.
  If, given that the offence is committed, the harm is certain or near-certain to occur, $p = 2$.

  (b) The C-score is the highest *hnp* value for all the harm-making properties of this type of offence.

(C4) If this type of offence satisfies C2 or C3 and is committed by two or more individuals in combination, and this offender is only an accomplice, as opposed to a ringleader, calculate the C-score using C2 or C3 and then halve it.

The S-score algorithm itself is simply the C-score algorithm plus the stipulation that the S-score for a given sentencing episode equals the sum of the C-scores for all the offence-types under consideration within it.

Taking into account the preliminary comments, I hope the S-score algorithm is reasonably easy to follow. However, it raises many questions, which I shall now endeavor to answer.

The C-score algorithm incorporates some ideas that are familiar from normal penal practice. It also has some very radical implications. In the next few pages I first select a couple of the conservative features and explain their utilitarian justification; I then explain and justify two very radical implications; finally, I examine some aspects that are more formal in nature.

Short-term harm

No penal system in the world attempts to punish every undesirable or immoral act. Most are just too minor to be worth the trouble. This feature is retained in the C-score algorithm. It is reflected in the fact that a tendency to create only short-term harm cannot in itself produce a C-score and therefore should not attract punishment. If this were not the case, we would have far too many offences to handle. For example, we cannot be expected to make a punitive response every time someone receives an insult which is not likely to have a *long-term* negative effect on her. However, when an act-type is likely to cause short-term harm and is *also* a *malum prohibitum*, it is punishable by clause C2 at a level of severity higher than a *malum prohibitum* that does not have this feature, for such a policy is not likely to lead to an overload.

Treatment of accomplices

C4 stipulates that when the act-type is carried out by several people in combination and the offender in question is an accomplice, as opposed to a ringleader, her C-score should be halved. This reflects standard penal practice in treating ringleaders more severely than accomplices. The utilitarian justification for it is that if an accomplice is deterred, the crime may still occur with a different accomplice (or possibly with no accomplice at all), whereas if a ringleader is deterred, then the crime is far less likely to occur (because the world does not contain so many potential ringleaders). Therefore, there is less value in deterring a potential accomplice than there is in deterring a potential ringleader.

Minimal use of statutes

The first respect in which the use of the S-score algorithm departs from normal judicial practice is the fact that it makes it unnecessary for every type of offence to be explicitly defined in statutory law. It may not have occurred to anyone to make it illegal to drop a T.V. set from the top floor of an office block so that it falls to a busy street below, but it is obvious to most people that this is a dangerous type of act and so, all other things being equal, it should be treated as punishable without this having to be explicitly written into the criminal law.[7] This has the advantage of sparing us the need to pre-define every type of offence in statute, and thus avoids the danger of certain kinds of clear offences just not being recognized. Admittedly, this is also the case in systems based on common law, rather than on statutes, but these have the extra complexity of having to identify relevant precedents as the basis for responding to each new offence.

In view of the foregoing, there is no need to pre-define offences such as murder or rape, whose harmfulness constitutes the reason for their criminality. According to the algorithm, there is no special offence of killing someone, but there is an offence of causing someone disastrous long-term harm, and killing may simply be regarded as the most extreme form of this. It might be asked why we do not at least punish killing more severely than lesser forms of disastrous harming. One answer to this is that we want to avoid additional complexity that would probably not yield much extra benefit in deterrent terms. Another answer is that it is not entirely clear that every instance of killing *is* an instance of disastrous harming—consider, for example, cases of euthanasia.

However, statutes cannot be dispensed with altogether. They are necessary, for example, in the case of *mala prohibita*, since a person cannot depend on her own sense of right and wrong to decide whether a particular sort of act would or would not be a *malum prohibitum*. Another type of situation where an explicit law is needed is in those cases where the vague word 'likely,' which appears in the definition of the probability p, needs clarification. This will be explained later (in the Gary Hart case study—see below, Sec. 5.4).

The irrelevance of actual consequences

The other major difference from conventional practice is less easily spotted, but obvious when pointed out. At least as far as *mala in se* are concerned, C-scores are independent of actual consequences. They depend only on the *tendency* of types of act to cause harm to people. It is irrelevant whether, on the occasion in question, the actual consequences were less serious or more serious than what we would expect in general. Indeed, it may be that the act has no harmful consequences at all on this occasion, but the C-score is a high one, reflecting the general dangerousness of this type of act. In this respect, the method accords with the observation made in Chapter One that what the agent deserves is based on what she believes prior to performing the act, and this may be only a probability, not a certainty, of harm. However, this link is really coincidental, for we are not concerned with deservingness here. Our reason for ignoring actual consequences is that it is necessary for *deterrent* purposes. What she cannot know until *after* she has performed a certain possible act cannot deter the potential agent of that act. And clearly she cannot know in advance the actual consequences of her act if these are different from what could have been predicted on the basis of general tendencies. When, for example, the state punishes an offender for causing the death of another by means of an act that could have been expected to have this result, it demonstrates a willingness to punish the perpetrators of future acts with the same tendency, not to punish perpetrators of acts which *turn out* to have the same result, for how can a potential offender know the consequences that her actions will turn out to have if these are different from their prospective likely consequences?

However, this reference to what an offender believes raises an important question. What are we to say about offenders who, for one reason or another, are ignorant of the tendencies of their actions? It seems we are driven here by two incompatible goals: firstly, the need for maximum deterrence; and secondly, the need for minimum *actual* punishment. (Both clearly serve the utilitarian aim of maximizing well-being.) At one extreme, we could threaten to punish the agents of all acts belonging to act-types whose harm-inducing tendencies are known by at least a small proportion of the population. This would give us a relatively high deterrent effect, since for all such act-types there would be some at least whose knowledge would enable them to be deterred by the threat. However, the cost would be the punishment of a large number of people who perform acts dangerous to others because they are ignorant of the danger involved. At the other extreme, we could threaten to punish only the agents of acts belonging to act-types whose harm-inducing tendencies are known by everyone, or almost everyone, in the population. This policy would obviously minimize the number of people who become punishable through ignorance, but it would lose us the opportunity of deterring some very dangerous actions.

There is no clear-cut solution to this problem. I shall say that our concern should be with actions whose dangerous tendencies are 'generally' known, where this term indicates a degree of prevalence of knowledge intermediate between the case of universality and that of knowledge by only a small group. The word is obviously very vague, but we shall have to live with this vagueness and the disagreements it is likely to give rise to in some cases. It is also worth noting that a government can—and perhaps should—increase the deterrent effect by publicizing examples of types of punishable acts and the C-scores associated with them. (Of course, the full S-score algorithm itself could be publicized, but this would be less easily grasped by most people.)

There is, however, one refinement that can be made which alleviates the problem just raised. There are some offenders who, because of their membership of a particular group, such as the medical profession, normally know more about the dangerous tendencies of certain sorts of acts than most people do. When such offenders are sentenced, this fact can be taken into account, and their S-scores may well increase as a result. If we adopt such a procedure, we will in the long run deter a greater number of dangerous acts than if we only ever appeal to the idea of what is 'generally known.' (How to incorporate this into the formal statement of the algorithm is demonstrated in the appendix.)

However, the appeal to what is generally known, whether in the population as a whole or within some smaller group, does not completely eliminate the difficulty. By punishing offenders when the presence of a danger of harming others would be generally known, we seem to be resurrecting the concept of 'negligence' rejected in Section 1.1; that is, we seem to be supposing that a person can be held responsible for doing what a 'reasonable person' would have recognized as wrong, even when he himself, not being 'reasonable,' does not recognize this. But it should be recalled in exactly what sense the concept of negligence was rejected in that section. We argued that in such a situation the person would not *deserve* unpleasant treatment for acting as she did. However, having become disillusioned with desert, we later adopted a utilitarian perspective, in which desert is treated as irrelevant from a normative point of view. From this perspective, it is sometimes necessary (I claim) to punish an offender who, at the time of the offence, did not know that her action was wrong—in other words, to operate, albeit in a very limited way, a policy of 'strict liability.' But this is a difficult matter, and best elucidated through suitable examples, which I shall supply in due course. (See below, Sec. 5.5.)

Using the highest hnp value

The algorithm bears some resemblance to the standard method of working out an expected utility, which involves multiplying each individual utility by its corresponding probability and adding together the resulting products. It is as if my algorithm were working out a measure of expected *disutility* for crimes. But one crucial difference is that the latter would require finding the sum of all the *hnp* values, rather than using the highest such value, as I propose. The reason for the difference lies in the fact that whereas the standard approach is intended to provide a theoretically watertight *definition* of expected utility, my algorithm is intended for practical use, and hence there needs to be a trade-off between theoretical accuracy and practical simplicity. I believe that in this case, simplicity should win out. It might be wondered, though, why I take the highest, as opposed to, say, the lowest *hnp* value. The reason is merely that it seems intuitively right. For example, if a single action risks serious injury to one person, but is also certain to inflict serious injury on a large number of people, it seems to make more intuitive sense to let the penalty be the higher one associated with the latter. Beyond that, I don't have a justification for this policy. The most important thing is to settle consistently on one policy or another.

Arbitrariness

Clearly there is a certain amount of arbitrariness in the C-score algorithm. The numbers could be different from what they are without necessarily producing an alternative that was any less 'correct.' There is no such thing as *the* correct algorithm. What matters here is to adopt an algorithm that is not clearly *incorrect* (which, for example, gives a lower C-score for an offence which is likely to cause disastrous harm than it gives for one that is likely to cause only non-disastrous harm). But once a certain option has been settled on, it is important that all judges stick to it to avoid unacceptable variation in sentencing and the loss of confidence that may then result.

'Coarseness'

The algorithm is 'coarser' than standard utilitarianism, in that it recognizes only three levels of harmfulness, only two levels for the number of people affected and only two levels for the probability of harm. Why is this? It is because, whatever the theoretical merits of a 'fine grained' system based on many levels, it would be too difficult to apply successfully. It would be too difficult to reach agreement about whether the harm involved was, say, a 4.2 or a 4.3. And it would be impossibly hard to agree about whether the probability of harm was, say, 0.65 or 0.7. If, in contrast, we use a very small range of numbers, each corresponding to an informal description, we are much more likely to achieve agreement. This is not to suggest that there will never be hard cases. For example, if there is danger of harm to precisely ten people, does this count as 'a limited number' or 'many'? In this case there is nothing to prevent us from adding further guidance. We could supplement the algorithm with a stipulation saying that, for example, a 'limited number' means 1 to 5, while 'many' means over 5. But we cannot do this in the case of the other two dimensions h and p, for there are no agreed ways of precisely measuring harmfulness, and although there is a standard way of expressing precise probabilities mathematically, it is not possible in practice to assign such precise probabilities in real-life situations of the sort encountered in a judicial system.

Specificity of action-types

It sometimes happens that an act belongs to a certain offence-type which, according to the algorithm, attracts a certain C-score, but also belongs to another offence-type that attracts a different C-score. For example, an act may belong to the offence-type of *mugging someone without violence*, which has a tendency to cause short-term harm and which, as a form of theft, is also a *malum prohibitum*, thus satisfying clause C2 and earning a C-score of 2. On the other hand, suppose the non-violent mugging was of an elderly person and so belonged to the offence-type *non-violent mugging of an elderly person*, which (we may suppose) has a tendency to cause more-or-less permanent psychological harm to the victim, and therefore satisfies clause C3, attracting a C-score of 4 ($h = 4$, $n = 1$, $p = 1$. $4 \times 1 \times 1 = 4$). It seems more reasonable to invoke the latter offence-type in describing the act rather than the former, since to use the former would be to omit important information. This is acceptable, I think, provided it satisfies the knowledge condition that I have proposed. If it is generally known[8] that mugging an elderly person, as opposed to a younger one, is likely to result in long-term harm to that person, then those contemplating this type of act are likely to know this, and therefore stand a reasonable chance of being deterred by the prospect of receiving a higher penalty. Otherwise, there can be no justification for invoking the more specific offence-type, and the penalty will have to be that associated with the broader one.

5.3 From S-scores to actual sentences

Having commented on a number of features of the S-score algorithm, I now want to turn to the important question of how S-scores are to be mapped onto actual punishments. I use imprisonment as my main example, because it is a widely used type of penalty and easily measurable in terms of the precise amount of time spent in jail, which in turn provides an indication of the severity of the punishment (only rough of course, because some people will cope much better with a given period of detention than others).

If P is the number of days in jail to which an offender is sentenced, and S is the offender's S-score, then it seems reasonable to relate P and S as follows:

$$P = KS$$

for some constant K. The choice of K determines how lenient or draconian the system of punishment will be. For example, if K is 10, then the most severe possible sentence for a single crime is 320 days, i.e., less than 1 year ($h = 8$, $n = 2$, $p = 2.8 \times 2 \times 2 \times 10 = 320$). This is obviously a very lenient system, at least by current day standards. If, on the other hand, K were to be set to 100, the maximum possible sentence would be 10 times as much = 3,200 days or nearly 9 years, which is much more severe. The choice of K is thus a crucial matter. I shall not recommend any particular value, as the decision has to be taken in the light of the best empirical evidence we have regarding the effectiveness of deterrence with different durations of detention, taking into account also their costs in terms of the effect on the offender and her family, but in view of the difficulties in obtaining solid empirical evidence, this is likely to leave viable a fairly wide range of possible values of K.

Another problem concerns the possibility of there being many offences under consideration in the same sentencing episode, leading to a large number of distinct C-scores and, in extreme cases, jail sentences that exceed the duration of a person's life-time (though this does depend of course on whether we have a large or a small value for K—it is more likely to happen in the former case). Actual jurisdictions tend to deal with this in one of two ways. The lenient way is to let the sentences run concurrently, so that the actual time served is no greater than the longest component sentence. The harsh way is simply to let the offender live out the rest of her life in jail. The former is not a good policy, in so far as it ignores the fact (pointed out by Bentham[9]) that an offender who has already decided to commit one offence needs to be given a reason, in the form of an increased penalty, to avoid committing another.[10] On the other hand, the latter could result in very many life sentences. One answer is to set an upper limit to all jail sentences—say, 10 years. In this case, a sentence of more than 10 years is simply not permitted in the deterrent system (unlike in the incapacitation system). The duration of a sentence will then be P (i.e. KS) or 10 X 365, whichever is the smaller. This gives some weight to Bentham's point without allowing excessively long deterrent sentences. However, it would still allow a situation in which an offender could receive quite a long sentence because of a large number of merely trivial offences, and this suggests that the problem is not just a matter of the absolute duration of sentences, but also (in some cases), their lack of proportion to the mildness of the component offences that generate them. So we may need a more nuanced system, which sets different upper limits depending on the size of the maximum C-score involved in the given sentencing episode. I shall not investigate the details of this here. I should emphasize that these complications will not need to be invoked very often if a small value of K is chosen for the system as a whole.

We must not overlook the fact that there are other types of penalties available to a criminal justice system besides imprisonment. Fines and community service orders are frequently used alternatives in modern states. This might seem to create another problem for my proposal. How are we to compare the severity value of, say, three weeks' community service with that of three weeks in jail? But the problem may only be apparent. On the whole, we will be using fines or community service orders for less serious offences, particularly for the sorts of *mala prohibita* that tend not to be directly harmful. We could in fact stipulate that any offender whose C-scores are limited to 1s (or in a slightly more lenient version, 1s and 2s) should receive a fine, community service order or suspended jail sentence.[11] Actual jail sentences could be reserved for those with higher component C-scores.[12] Now there is of course a certain range of severity in lighter penalties themselves, and my algorithm does not help us in the task of proportioning the level of severity to the seriousness of the *malum prohibitum* (except perhaps where we assign a tougher penalty to one that is accompanied by a risk of short-term harm). Some additional principle might be developed to allow this to be done. On the other hand, we may be able to live with a certain amount of judicial unpredictability here, as the sentences concerned are all fairly mild in any case.

In the course of the above discussion, I have suggested a number of refinements to deal with various problems. There may well be other problems with the system that simply have not occurred to me. With a procedure of this kind, it would be necessary to test it for a period of time to see what difficulties arise and to make such further refinements as may be needed. After this, it can be implemented on a strict basis, with all judges required to follow it to the letter,

5.4 Case studies for the application of the algorithm

Here are the three cases studies promised earlier. The first one is a case we have already examined in relation to desert; we study it now for the light it can throw on the implications of our new 'desert-free' approach.

Gary Hart

The facts in the Gary Hart case were covered in Chapter One, and do not need repeating here. The sentencing episode seemed to involve at worst one type of offence—that of driving while sleepy. This earns a C-score of 8, because it is a type of offence likely to result in disastrous harm for a limited number of individuals. ($h = 8, n = 1, p = 1$. $8 \times 1 \times 1 = 8$.) As there were no other offences being considered, the S-score would also be 8. Note that this type of offence creates only a *danger* of disastrous harm, not a certainty or near-certainty of it. (Hence the decision to set p to 1 rather than 2.)

Some might question the use of the word 'likely' in relation to the harm that may be caused by an act of this sort. In fact, the chance of serious harm being caused by a single act of driving while sleepy may be quite small.[13] There are a huge number of types of acts which similarly carry a small chance of disastrously harming someone, but their propensity to do so is not obvious to a great number of people. It is therefore necessary for the state to publicize those that are going to be considered grounds for punishment, and this can be done by means of statutes. (Many of them will be specialized to particular fields of activity, e.g., driving vehicles or selling perishable food.) To fail to do this would essentially amount to the extreme policy rejected above, in which one punishes the perpetrators of all acts whose dangerousness would be known by at least a small proportion of the population. So for each such type of act, the state must make a formal declaration if it wishes to treat it as punishable, and furthermore, a period of 'amnesty' should be allowed to permit citizens to become aware of the new law.[14]

Returning to Gary Hart, note how the fact that ten people died as a result of Hart's actions has no effect on his C-score or S-score. The general (and highly radical) implications of this approach should be obvious. Any person who is found to have been driving while sleepy may be punished on the basis of an S-score typically equal to at least 8. Similarly for drunken drivers and others engaged in acts 'officially' recognized as dangerous, *whether or not any harm is actually done*. It hardly needs pointing out that such an approach would need a considerable re-adjustment of attitudes on the part of the general public.

If K is set to 10, Gary Hart would be sentenced to 8 X 10 = 80 days in jail. If K is set to 100, he would be sentenced to 8 X 100 = 800 days, or about 2 years 2 months. Only for much higher values of K would he receive anything approaching the five years that he actually got. But given that there is considerable uncertainty about what the correct value of K should be, the real message that we should learn from this case study is not about what actual sentence he should have received, but the fact that according to the S-score algorithm, he should have received no less and no more than someone who behaved in the same way but was lucky enough to do no harm. And in this respect the use of the S-score algorithm is, I argue, quite justified, for it reflects our exclusive concern with deterrence in that part of the penal system in which it is intended to operate.

Union Carbide and Bhopal

> In the middle of the night of December 2-3, 1984, residents living near the Union Carbide pesticide plant in Bhopal, India awoke coughing, choking, gasping, and in the case of thousands, slowly dying. Half a day later, half a world away, company executives sleeping soundly near the Danbury, CT headquarters of Union Carbide Corporation awoke in the middle of the night yawning and grumbling at the sound of telephones ringing. . . . shortcuts taken in the name of profit—authorized by the highest executives within the company—had just killed thousands of innocent citizens. It was the worst industrial disaster of the 20th century, forever changing the public's trust of the chemical industry. Union Carbide claimed it was sabotage by a disgruntled employee that led to the disaster, but how much did the company already know about the dangerous conditions its shortcuts and bottom-line focus had created? (www.chemicalindustryarchives.org/dirtysecrets/bhopal/index.asp)

As in the case of Gary Hart, I will not make controversial factual assertions and will therefore not endorse the account given above. I merely want to ask how we should apply the S-score algorithm *if* the facts are as stated.

In Section 3.5 I argued that corporate punishment was an unjustified practice and that punishment should always be directed at individuals. Let us suppose, for the sake of argument, that several individuals within Union Carbide got together to approve designs whose implementation they knew would risk injury and death to a large number of people. (This hypothesis does not entail that they *intended* such risk.) And let us further suppose that one of these individuals was particularly dominant in the making of this decision, while the others, although they played crucial roles, largely followed his lead.

Consider the dominant individual first. He performed an act of a sort that is likely to cause disastrous harm to a large number of individuals, and so his C-score (and hence his S-score, assuming that there were no other relevant offences) should be 16 according to C3. ($h = 8$, $n = 2$, $p = 1$. $8 \times 2 \times 1 = 16$.) With $K = 10$, this equates to 160 days or about 5 months in jail. With $K = 100$, it gives 1,600 days or about 4 years 5 months in jail.

As far as the 'accomplices' are concerned, the calculation is the same, except that the C-score (and hence the S-score, assuming no further offences) is halved in accordance with C4, with the effect that the sentence is half that imposed on the 'ringleader.'[15]

Incidentally, we can see here a serious weakness with the idea of corporate responsibility, which is precisely that it does not distinguish between ringleaders and accomplices. According to this notion, all members of the corporation share equally in responsibility for the actions concerned, which is hardly satisfactory from the point of view of deterrence—or fair retribution, come to that.

The fact that thousands of people *actually* died is not relevant to the determination of the S-scores of these individuals. However, it is very important for something else—compensating the injured survivors and relatives for their loss. I do accept that it is reasonable for compensation to be made to the victims, and that this should be done as far as possible from the funds of the convicted individuals—and that would be in addition to any penalty imposed by the deterrent system of punishment based on S-scores.[16]

Looking at the S-scores that we have assigned to the offenders in the Bhopal tragedy, some may think that it does not do justice to the scale of the wrongdoing. According to the extract above, the incident was the worst industrial disaster of the twentieth century. I have assigned to the 'ringleader' an S-score of 16, twice that of Gary Hart for his (alleged) wrongdoing in the Selby incident, and to the 'accomplices,' an S-score of 8, only equal to Hart's. Yet the scale of death and injury was far more than twice that caused by Hart. Surely, it might be argued, this is not truly proportionate punishment.

This has much to do with the algorithm's handling of the 'numbers of people affected' parameter, which is confined to distinguishing only between a 'limited' number of people and a 'large' number. It could have been designed in a more directly utilitarian way with n set to the actual number of people that would have been expected to be harmed. However, when we are dealing with probabilities rather than certainties, it is impossible to calculate such a number in practice. Also, it seems unlikely that greater accuracy, even if it could be achieved, would have any genuine benefit in deterrent terms. Of course, those who urge this objection are likely not to be thinking purely in such terms. They may think that the penalty proposed is so light as to be retributively unjust. But that consideration has no weight now.

Myra Hindley

Myra Hindley was jailed in 1966, along with Ian Brady, after being convicted of the murders of Lesley Ann Downey, aged 10, in 1964 and Edward Evans, aged 17, in 1965 (http://news.bbc.co.uk/1/hi/uk/4582430.stm). The depravity involved in these crimes was extreme, including abduction and torture. On the other hand, Hindley seemed to be very much the 'disciple' of Brady, who had influenced her through his personality and amoral views.

The first question to ask is whether Hindley is to be classified as a very dangerous offender, i.e., one who was extremely likely to re-offend in a very serious manner, which would bring her under the incapacitating system, giving her a choice between lifetime confinement and state-assisted suicide, or a more 'normal' criminal, which would bring her under the deterrent-based system. The answer to this question mainly turns on a matter which has been much discussed over the years—whether Hindley was intrinsically capable of committing these crimes on her own, or whether instead she acted only under the influence of Brady.[17] In the former case, it would seem right to regard her as a very dangerous offender and to treat her accordingly; in the latter, such a course would have no justification, and she would have to be considered more suited to the deterrent-based system. While incarcerated, Hindley did start to claim that she was a reformed person, and she had at least one eminent individual, Lord Longford, to support her in this. But it is very difficult to know how much reliance one can put upon such claims (which is not to suggest that they should be dismissed out of hand).

As my purpose here is to illustrate the more complex deterrent-based system, I shall just assume, for purely heuristic purposes, that Hindley *did* act solely under the influence of Brady, and that this influence was transient—soon after contact ended between them, she returned to morality and to more acceptable behavioral dispositions and, crucially, would have done so even if she had not been incarcerated. This would be sufficient to justify bringing her under the deterrent-based system—not to deter Hindley herself from future wrongdoing, since *ex hypothesi* she was reformed, but rather as a contribution to general deterrence.

For each of the two crimes for which Hindley was convicted, there were three distinct acts (abducting, torturing and killing), each requiring its own separate C-score. Of the three acts, only the killing has an immediately obvious h-value, namely 8. What is the h-value of abducting a child? I suggest 4, since it would be likely to cause some long-term, but not necessarily disastrous, trauma. The same presumably applies to the act of torturing a child, which therefore also receives 4 (as long as the torture is not life-threatening, or likely to cause the kind of injuries that would ruin a person's whole life).

The C-scores for the acts of abducting, torturing and killing are therefore, respectively: 4 X 1 X 1 X 0.5= 2; 4 X 1 X 1 X 0.5= 2; and 8 X 1 X 2 X 0.5 = 8. (Each score is halved at the end because of Hindley's accomplice status.) There were two offences, each with the given list of C-scores, so to get the S-score, calculate 2 X 2 X 2 X 8 = 64. For $K = 10$, this gives a jail sentence of 64 X 10 = 640 days, i.e., about 1 year 9 months. For $K = 100$, the jail sentence is 64 X 100 = 6,400 days or about 17 years 7 months.

Some may feel that even seventeen and a half years is too lenient for Hindley. They may think this because they regard Hindley as a very dangerous offender. This would be going against my assumption that Hindley would never have offended had it not been for Brady's influence. I do not know that this assumption is true, and if it is not, then I can agree that lifetime confinement (or state-assisted suicide if she chose it) would have been more suitable for her. Other critics of my recommendation may be thinking that seventeen and a half years is less than what she *deserved*, but again, this is not a consideration that we can allow ourselves to invoke at this point.

5.5   Exculpation

It is recognized in all criminal justice systems that there are sometimes grounds for reducing the sentence that would normally be required, or even for exculpating the offender entirely. Can either of these features be incorporated into my system without having to say that the offender did not really 'deserve' the punishment that the system would normally dictate? I am talking here about the deterrent-based part—the incapacitating part does not admit of exceptions, once the extreme dangerousness of the offender is established.

Remember first that we always have a presumptive reason not to punish—punishment is distressing, and sometimes permanently harmful to its victim. So if we *can* avoid it, we will want to do so. The constraint that we must meet if we do not punish (or punish less severely than we otherwise would have) is that this must not damage deterrence—or at least, it must not damage it enough to outweigh the avoidance of harm in not punishing or in punishing less. Of course, there is a great deal of guesswork in this, as there is in all matters affecting the well-being of large groups of people.

What I propose to do is present a series of eight fictional (but I think plausible) examples, in which some sort of case can be made for not punishing the agent, despite her having acted badly. In some cases I will support and justify the judgment that there should be no punishment; in others I will reject it and affirm the need to punish. I shall start with the most incontrovertible cases, and lead gradually to those in which the case for exculpation is more questionable. In the course of discussing the various cases, a rationale for exculpation will emerge, which, I believe, adequately balances the interests of the offender with the interests of society in general, and this will be explicitly stated about halfway through.

Monica

Monica is a bank cashier. A man enters the bank where she is working, and demands that she hand over a substantial sum of cash, revealing to Monica (but not to anyone else in the bank) that he has a shotgun. Monica hands over the money.

This case is straightforward, in fact almost trivial. Monica will not be punished because, though in general we want to discourage bank cashiers from handing over the bank's money to strangers, we do not want to do so in the special case where the cashier has good reason to think that if she does not hand it over, she may be killed. And the reason for *this* is that to hand over someone else's money to a third party if the only alternative is one's death is not even morally wrong—it represents a standard type of exception to the general principle that stealing or abetting a theft is morally wrong. It is recognized as an exception (the utilitarian would claim) because, though tolerating theft in general would lead to very bad consequences, the consequences of not 'abetting' the theft in this particular kind of case would be catastrophically bad for the person concerned, and we can make the exception without endangering general conformity to the principle.[18]

Bill

Now consider Bill, a person with learning difficulties, who points a gun at someone and fires it, causing that person's death. Because of his learning difficulties, Bill did not really understand the likely consequences of what he was doing. If Bill did not have learning difficulties, we might have no difficulty in calling his act murder. Applying our algorithm to this case will give Bill a C-score of 16. ($h = 8, n = 1, p = 2. 8 \times 1 \times 2 = 16$.) But surely, one is likely to protest, there is a good reason for not punishing Bill at all, which is that he did not understand what he was doing. This appears intuitively right from a retributive point of view, for Bill seems to lack the element of moral responsibility that the retributivist deems necessary for desert of punishment. But of course, we are not admitting retributive reasons as adequate grounds for determining the appropriateness or otherwise of punishment. We need a justification in terms of deterrence, or rather lack of it.

Suppose Bill *is* acquitted because of his learning difficulties. Imagine Jim, who does not have learning difficulties, and who is contemplating murder, finding out about Bill's exculpation and the reason for it. Even if Jim has never previously heard of Bill, it is hardly surprising that this should happen, since convictions and acquittals will normally be publicized, along with justifying reasons. So Jim knows that Bill was let off because of his learning difficulties. Assuming that the prospect of punishment weighs with Jim at all (and if it does not, then Jim's case is irrelevant here), is it likely to have *less* force because he knows of Bill's acquittal, together with the fact that it was due to Bill's learning difficulties? The answer is surely no. Jim knows that he himself does not have learning difficulties. Perhaps he could convince the judge that he did. But he is in fact very unlikely to embark on such a strange—and almost certainly hopeless—act of attempted deceit. It would therefore seem safe to say that any deterrent effect on Jim of possible punishment for murder would be most unlikely to be lessened by his knowledge of Bill's case. And similarly with almost all other would-be murderers who know of such cases. So Bill's exculpation would surely not harm deterrence, and is therefore quite justified.

Gemma

A new law has been introduced requiring all children below a certain age to use a safety seat when traveling in a car. The new law has been given wide publicity, and so very few people are unaware of it. However, Gemma, who has a child below this age, has been out of the country for the six months since the publicity for the new law began. She therefore does not know of the existence of the law. On returning to this country, she takes her child for a car ride without putting him in a safety seat. According to the S-score algorithm, she will then incur a C-score of 8. ($h = 8, n = 1, p = 1. 8 \times 1 \times 1 = 8$.) But this hardly seems fair. She did not know that the law existed—and for a very good reason. There is of course the adage that 'ignorance of the law is no excuse,' but in a case like Gemma's, we are inclined to feel more sympathy. Let us assume, in accordance with this intuition, that Gemma, though caught, is exculpated on the grounds that she was ignorant of the relevant law.

Now Rodrigo is contemplating taking *his* child for a car drive. He knows about the new law. Unfortunately, he hasn't got a safety seat available, and he has no time to obtain one before the journey. He knows about Gemma, who was let off because of her ignorance of the law. Rodrigo is *not* ignorant of the law. But perhaps, if caught, he could *feign* ignorance—surely he would have a good chance of getting away with it. So it seems that letting Gemma off was a bad idea from the point of view of deterrence. People like Rodrigo, who know perfectly well what they are doing, but think it possible that they might be caught, would not take the threat of punishment seriously, provided only that they thought they could get away with lying.

Are we therefore forced to punish Gemma? That would be unfortunate. A way out of our quandary might be to adopt a *high standard of proof* whenever it is claimed that a person offended out of mere ignorance. In effect, there would need to be something unusual about the offender's case that would persuade us that ignorance had indeed been the reason. In Gemma's case it would be the unusual circumstance of her being out of the country for such a lengthy period of time (which should of course be easily provable) that would convince us that she was ignorant of the new law. In addition, we can make it very clear to the general public that unless one has strong proof of this kind, one's plea of ignorance will not be accepted. So *just claiming* that one was ignorant without any further support would not be good enough. Of course, this does have the drawback that those who offend out of ignorance, but are not lucky enough to have convincing proof of this will still be punished, which seems unfair. But the alternatives (either excusing *no* ignorant offender, which in open-and-shut cases like Gemma's seems absurd, or else excusing any offender who can make some sort of case for ignorance, however dubious, and thus risking many fraudulent claims) seem to me worse.

Joanna

Joanna is a virtual slave to Arnold, who keeps her permanently locked up. He visits her occasionally to rape and torture her. This has been going on for months. Joanna has been unable to alert the outside world to her plight. One day, however, while Arnold is out, she manages to get hold of a knife. When he returns, she plunges the knife into him, causing his death. She is then able to escape.

Most people would feel great sympathy for Joanna and would not want her to be found guilty of murder—indeed, they would probably want her acquitted altogether. According to the S-score algorithm, Joanna should receive a score of 16. ($h = 8$, $n = 1$, $p = 2$.) Can we override this and exonerate her without weakening general deterrence in relation to murder?

I think we can justify exoneration by arguing that in her unusual circumstances, to kill Arnold was not even morally wrong. Not every act of killing is immoral. In general, we are not required to desist from killing others when it would be necessary to end a genuinely intolerable situation. This was Joanna's position. Killing Arnold was almost like an act of self-defense and carried with it more-or-less the same grounds for leniency. It is true that deterrence will be weakened slightly by exculpating Joanna. Others contemplating acts of killing whose special circumstances would render such killing morally acceptable will know that they too will be exculpated, and so will not be deterred—but that is fine, for we do not want them to be deterred, precisely because their acts of killing would not be morally wrong—indeed, perhaps we should even *want* them to kill in such cases. Of course, it is possible that some potential murderers may think that their act would be morally acceptable when it would not be, but as long as it is made clear to people that such exculpation will be limited to the very rare cases of the sort described here, this will rarely happen, if at all.

Anita

But now consider Anita, whose situation resembles Joanna's in some respects. Anita is a battered wife. She has been enduring violent abuse from her husband for many years, but she feels attached to him, and cannot bear to leave him. However, one day she reaches the point where the anger that she feels towards him boils over, and she attacks and kills him.

Although there are clearly some important differences between Joanna's and Anita's situations (principally the fact that Joanna cannot escape her tormentor, whereas Anita can), we tend to react to both in somewhat similar ways. We are sure that Joanna should not be punished for killing her captor, and many of us are scarcely less sure that Anita should not be punished for killing her partner. We feel immense sympathy for both women and a wish for both to be able to put their awful experiences behind them. We may also feel some retributive anger on behalf of each woman vis-à-vis their respective tormentors. This, however, needs to be suppressed, in so far as we are able to achieve this. Additionally, we may feel some political bias of a feminist kind, but this needs to be suppressed as well.[19]

In so far as it is not produced by such biases, the sympathy that we feel for each woman is certainly morally appropriate but, as in every case we have so far examined, there is something else to consider—the effect that exculpation would have on the effectiveness of the deterrent system. We have already done this in Joanna's case, and we were satisfied that there would be no significant danger of its being weakened if she were excused punishment. But can we reach the same conclusion in Anita's case? The fact that Anita can get away from her partner, that she can, if necessary, separate from him for good, seems to make her case crucially different from Joanna's. If we acquit Anita of murder, are we not sending a message to the public that it is acceptable to kill a tormentor of this sort even if you have the much more morally acceptable option of simply putting yourself beyond his reach?

But should we really be saying that Anita had *options*? We argued in Chapter Two that, owing to determinism, people are able to do only what they *actually* do. Since what Anita actually did was to kill her partner, we must then say that she was unable to do anything else.[20] In view of this, how can it be right to punish her? The general conclusion would be that since the behavior of every person is determined, no person ever deserves punishment for any offence that she may commit, and therefore punishment is always wrong. Obviously I do not accept this view, but it is worth reiterating why not. It is because even if desert does create a presumptive reason for punishing offenders (something that we questioned in any case), lack of desert merely removes that presumptive reason, but there can be other presumptive reasons, e.g., that if one does not punish, the relevant offences will be committed more often than if one does.

But in the case of Anita and others in similar situations, this stance may appear unrealistic. When she lashes out at her partner, Anita is probably not thinking rationally. She is not in a position to contemplate the fact that she could achieve her aims just as effectively, and in a more morally acceptable way, by simply leaving him. Consequently, it can be argued that Anita and those similarly situated cannot be deterred by the thought of criminal sanctions. However, we face an epistemic problem here. How can we be certain that Anita's state of anger was sufficiently controlling that it deprived her temporarily of her rational faculties? It could be that her action was actually more calculating than she or her lawyer will probably claim. If exculpation on grounds of uncontrollable anger were permitted, it would soon be applied to a large range of cases in which it was not implausible to think that the offender may have felt such anger. The excuse would become common, resulting in many acquittals, with the likely effect that those contemplating murder would often think the chances of acquittal if caught were high. There is a contrast here between Anita's case and Bill's. Bill's learning difficulties are plain for everyone to see. Because there is no epistemic problem associated with it, the act of exculpating Bill because of these difficulties will not lead to a large number of acquittals in which defendants and lawyers in effect exploit the presence of uncertainty.

It might be thought that instead of acquitting Anita altogether, we should reduce her sentence—this would at least allow us to convey sympathy for her plight while maintaining deterrence at least to some extent. But surely our sympathy is best expressed simply by a statement from the judge. Reducing the sentence would create a precedent that may eventually lead to the erosion of the system of proportionality. In general, I do not see a role for *mitigation*, as opposed to complete exculpation, in state punishment systems. Either an exception can be made without damaging deterrence or it cannot. In the former case, acquittal is required. In the latter, the offender should be punished as normal.

Perhaps we can now begin to discern certain general principles governing the advisability of exculpation. It seems that the following conditions should be satisfied:

(1) Each type of case, and the characteristics of the offender involved, should be such that *either*:

   (a) the offender clearly could not have been deterred by the threat of punishment;[21]

   or

   (b) the relevant action was clearly not wrong.

(2) A deceptive claim that an offender satisfied the relevant characteristics would be almost impossible to make convincing, and this would be obvious to almost anyone who might consider trying.

(3) The total number of such cases is a small proportion of all cases, so as to minimize the weakening of deterrence.

With these principles in mind, let us now resume our examination of the different kinds of cases in which exculpation might be thought reasonable.

Alison

Alison is a single mother who has been caught stealing clothes for her needy children from a supermarket. Should she be punished?

This was an example from Duff that we discussed earlier in connection with the consequences of utilitarian punishment for the marginalized. It was left unresolved at that point. Can we make any further progress with the concepts that we have developed since then?

The most promising route would perhaps be to assimilate Alison's case to that of Joanna. We concluded that Joanna should not be punished because, although killing someone is normally wrong and punishable, it was not so in Joanna's particular situation. Can we similarly argue that although stealing is normally wrong and punishable, it was not so in Alison's circumstances? After all, Alison needs to provide clothes for her children. True, it is possible that she has other options. She might, for example, be able to obtain state benefits. But state benefits are rarely adequate to cover all necessities. So it is conceivable that Alison had no reasonable alternative to stealing the clothes. Should we not then conclude that it was morally acceptable for her to do this, and therefore constituted behavior that we should not wish to deter in her or others similarly situated?

There would be some worries about taking this line. The category of case could perhaps be described as 'stealing to obtain necessities that cannot be obtained in any other way.' As we have suggested, it is plausible to suppose that this is not immoral and therefore that condition (1b) is satisfied. However, it is sometimes feasible to successfully represent one's financial situation as more desperate than it really is, making it doubtful that condition (2) is satisfied. Also, because of difficulties in fixing precisely what is encompassed by the term 'necessities,' there is the risk of a slippery slope that may result in violation of condition (3). It therefore seems dangerous to recognize this category as a type of case for legitimate exculpation.

Admittedly, this seems odd. Apparently, we are saying that an action can be morally acceptable and yet appropriate for punishment to protect society in general. This is regrettably true. There is both an epistemic problem and a problem about public perception. The epistemic problem concerns the question of whether we can be sure that the feature that accounts for the action's moral acceptability—in this case the financial desperateness of the agent—is really present. The problem of public perception is the likelihood of acquittal on these grounds becoming common, so that many people are encouraged to seek it, with resulting serious damage to deterrence. So our conclusion appears correct. There may indeed be a sense in which punishing such agents is unjust and opponents of utilitarian ethics are likely to make much of this. However, two points can be made in response. Firstly, if hard determinism is right, it is no more unjust than any other punishment, since every punishment is suffering inflicted on someone who does not deserve it. Secondly, the C-score for this offence would probably only be 1 (for a *malum prohibitum* causing no significant harm) and would most likely lead only to a short community service order.

Joshua

Up until recently, Joshua was a morally good person, something that he repeatedly demonstrated in his behavior. But he recently injured his head, and since then his behavior has turned unexpectedly vicious. In particular, he attacked someone who had been his long-term friend. This is something he would never have done before his injury. It is interesting also that when executing this crime, Joshua deliberately (albeit unsuccessfully) disguised himself in an attempt to avoid being identified.

Joshua appears to have suffered some sort of brain injury which has affected his moral sense, causing him to perform a callous and immoral act. Putting the matter in conventional terms, Joshua is not morally responsible for his action and it might therefore be thought wrong to punish him. However, what matters is whether the three general conditions identified above are satisfied if his brain injury is offered as a reason for exculpation. For condition (1) to be satisfied, either (1a) or (1b) must hold. (1b) definitely does not hold, as there is no question of our treating Joshua's action as morally acceptable. Therefore, (1a) must hold for exculpation to be allowable. But there is considerable doubt about whether it does hold. The question is whether Joshua's brain injury made it impossible for him to be deterred by the threat of punishment. Now clearly Joshua was *not* deterred, for he did commit the crime. But was deterrence *impossible* in his case? This is another of those questions that seem confusing in the context of an outlook that accepts hard determinism. We need to recall why we are interested in this question. We want to ensure that deterrence is not significantly weakened. It might be significantly weakened if exculpation of Joshua would lead other potential offenders who knew about it and knew also that they themselves had a similar brain injury would fail to be deterred by the general threat of punishment when they otherwise would have been. And this is very likely to be the case. It might *not* be the case if such brain injuries rendered deterrence impossible, e.g., because they rendered the agent completely irrational—something that we know does not apply to Joshua, particularly in view of his deliberate attempt to avoid being identified. From this I think we can see how to interpret the word 'impossible' in the question 'Was deterrence impossible?' It is to be understood *epistemically,* so that we will treat deterrence as possible in the agent's particular circumstances only if we do not know of any reason why these circumstances would prevent deterrence. Since we know of no such reason in the case of someone in Joshua's condition, we will say that deterrence *is* possible and so condition (1a) is not satisfied. Hence Joshua should be punished as the normal operation of the system would dictate (but not in such a way as to undermine appropriate medical help for his condition). Of course, Joshua does not *deserve* punishment. It was not his fault that he underwent a brain injury which (in combination no doubt with other factors) caused him to harm another person. But, as we have already argued many times, lack of desert does not override the good reasons, mainly concerned with deterrence, which we may have for punishing someone. Again, we may feel *sympathy* for Joshua as a result of his punishment. But such sympathy is appropriate for *anyone* who is punished, and it does not provide a good reason for not punishing if the utilitarian reasons for doing so are sound and compelling.

Tim

Tim has killed someone in what appeared to be a calculated act. Like Joshua, he made an attempt to avoid being identified as the killer, but failed. Tim has not suffered any head injury, nor has there been any other kind of verifiable event or state that could explain Tim's act. However, an eminent psychiatrist testifies that Tim is suffering from a mental disorder. It seems he hallucinates voices telling him to commit murder. Should Tim be acquitted on grounds of insanity?

If Tim is really hearing voices, could their influence be so strong that he is unable to resist it? Translating this into terms conformable to hard determinism: are they so strong that we *know* that someone hearing such voices will do what they command him to do? That doesn't seem very plausible, casting doubt on whether condition (1a) is satisfied. Nor is it at all plausible to suppose that (1b) is satisfied, as Tim's act was clearly immoral. Furthermore, it would surely not be too difficult for a determined fraudster to persuade a psychiatrist that such things were happening to him when they were not. Therefore condition (2) is not satisfied either. And there may also be the problem that because genuine insanity is often hard to diagnose, there will be a temptation to let it cover more and more cases, a slippery slope effect that casts doubt on the satisfaction of condition (3). (We see this particularly in the U.S., where the plea of insanity in homicide cases seems to have become almost routine.) Based on these considerations, I think we should conclude that Tim should not in fact be acquitted.

5.6 State punishment: concluding remarks

Before leaving the subject of state punishment, I want to draw a lesson about the proper treatment of desert within utilitarianism—or rather reinforce an earlier lesson. In Section 4.4 I argued that utilitarians should jettison the concept of moral desert, instead of trying to absorb it into utilitarian theory. I think that this has now been further confirmed by consideration of some of the examples in the previous section, Joshua and Tim in particular. For we are unlikely to think that these two people deserve their punishments, and yet it is not true, according to my utilitarian view, that they should be excused. Of course, some will claim that this conclusion weakens my case, rather than strengthening it, for most of us are unlikely to feel comfortable about punishing these individuals in opposition to our intuition that they do not deserve it. But I would remind such critics that in the case of people incorrectly punished because of a miscarriage of justice—which is bound to happen occasionally even in the best run system—we have people being punished without deserving it. Yet few would think this a sufficient reason for not having any criminal justice system. (If they did, they would have to contend with the arguments of Chapter Four, particularly those connected with the need to avoid a collapse of civil society.)

I have described my treatment of utilitarian state punishment as 'detailed,' and indeed I believe it is more so than many other accounts. However, it does not cover every aspect. Any system that is intended for practical use is bound to require more elaboration than the outline provided here. I should perhaps add that owing to its radical nature, I do not expect anything like it to be implemented in any country in the near future. For the time being, it is best viewed as a source of ideas which, I believe, are worth advocating when the question of reforming any existing system is on the table.

Finally, I think it is worth pointing out that the central problem of determining the correct punitive response for different sorts of offences and offenders, which has been my concern here, is not the only problem of state punishment that may benefit from philosophical scrutiny. Another problem, and perhaps an even more pressing one from a practical point of view, has to do with ascertaining precisely what (if anything) given offenders have done that may require punishment. Is the standard of 'proof beyond reasonable doubt' a sensible one? What exactly does it mean, and do juries typically understand its meaning? (Do judges?) Such questions have important philosophical aspects, but are beyond the scope of this book.

5.7 Punishment within the family

In the final section of this chapter I wish to redress slightly the imbalance that has hitherto resulted in state punishment being viewed as practically the sole kind of punishment. I shall consider one particular form of non-judicial punishment—that inflicted on children by their parents or guardians.

Clearly, we can raise exactly the same crucial question about this sort of punishment as we have done about the state-inflicted variety: since punishment, by its very nature, is intended to cause pain or distress, what is its moral justification? Is it even right to assume that punishment of children by their parents is *ever* justified? Many argue that it isn't, believing that other methods should be used for correcting errant children, such as simply talking to them about the wrongness of their behavior and setting a good example by one's own actions. But anyone who has ever tried to bring up children knows that there is simply no avoiding some acts of punishment. Talking is often ineffective, as young children frequently have difficulty understanding the full meaning of what is said to them, and even when they do understand it, their conformity cannot always be expected as a consequence, any more than in the case of adults. Setting a good example is highly desirable, since children often mimic their parents' behavior—indeed, a great deal of their learning takes this form—but they may not always see the relevance of the example to themselves or, if they do, may have overwhelmingly strong desires that override it. In contrast, threatening to impose some mild penalty on a child if she is naughty (e.g., canceling a planned trip), together with a consistent policy of following up on such threats when necessary, can be effective.

But this reference to 'effectiveness' doesn't fully answer the question about justification. It is certainly true that one can often effect a change in a child's behavior by means of punishment, but *ought* one to do so? It is very tempting for parents to use punishment to enforce a child's conformity with whatever they—the parents—happen to want. If, for example, they want peace and quiet rather than hearing the sound of their children playing, it might be tempting for them to use punishment to enforce this. But, assuming that the play is of a normal, non-harmful sort and that the *only* reason for objecting to it is its noisiness, it is far from obvious that the parents would be acting in a morally acceptable way in such a case.

The principal moral justification for parents' punishing their children surely lies in the probable long-term harm to the child (and perhaps to others) if they do not eliminate various undesirable patterns of behavior from their child's character, coupled with the impossibility or impracticality of other means of achieving this. The first point is uncontroversial, while the second was defended above by reference to the common experience of parents.

Of course, none of this entails that punishment should in every situation be regarded as the only, or the best, means of controlling a child's behavior. Because of the distress caused to the child, and because it may even appear to set her a poor example of adult insensitivity or callousness, alternatives to punishment, such as rewards for good behavior and reasoned argument, should always be used instead whenever they are likely to be effective.

Besides the general question of justification, there is also the issue of the method or means of punishment. Most of the controversy concerns corporal (physical) punishment. Beating children has been a common practice throughout history,[22] but has, particularly in recent years, aroused moral revulsion. It implies treating children in a way that it would never be permissible to treat an adult (i.e., assaulting them) and, to those concerned with children's rights, appears symbolic of adults' somewhat unbalanced and hegemonic position with respect to young people. Indeed, the issue of corporal punishment has dominated the public discussion of children's rights perhaps more than any other. Many countries have gone as far as legally proscribing the practice.

But in point of fact, the term corporal punishment covers a wide range of practices, from a light slap to a ferocious caning. Nobody would seriously suggest that all of these are of equal moral gravity. It would surely be quite wrong to treat mild smacking as if it were as bad as brutal beating with a cane. This sort of distinction is effectively recognized in British law, which allows only 'reasonable chastisement' of children. Yet many continue to support the position of those countries that have outlawed corporal punishment altogether. Certainly a complete ban has the merit of simplicity and avoids the need for interpreting the vague word 'reasonable' in borderline cases. However, it risks criminalizing behavior, which, even if wrong, is surely too trivial to be a matter of judicial concern.

Furthermore, some defenders of corporal punishment claim that it has particular advantages as compared with other kinds of punishment available to parents. It can be administered as an immediate and quick response to the offence, something that will be remembered by the child, but is not dragged out.

While there may be some truth to this, I think that there is a particular danger with corporal punishment that does not apply to most other ways of punishing children. It is that when inflicted by a person in a state of anger, corporal punishment clearly runs the risk of going too far and causing injury. In extreme cases, corporal punishment inflicted in anger can, and occasionally has, resulted in death. Defenders would doubtless recognize this, but deduce only that corporal punishment should *not* be inflicted in anger; they would say it should only ever be the result of calm deliberation. However, anger, by its very nature, is blind to its own consequences, and corporal punishment, if it is allowed to become habitual, will sooner or later, in a quick-tempered person, lead to quite dangerous situations.

This is reason enough, I think, for discouraging the corporal punishment of children. But are those countries who have taken disapproval to the point of criminalization justified in doing so? Conventional state punishment recognizes the legitimacy of punishing some types of act because of their *potential* to cause harm, rather than because they are certain to do so, and I have generally endorsed this. (Indeed, in my system potential harm, rather than actual harm, is the key to legal culpability). But the problem is that those who are *not* quick-tempered with their children and use mild corporal punishment in the process of bringing them up in a generally loving and responsible way, will find it difficult to understand why they are being subjected to a law that exists primarily to control those who, as parents, are not so well-adjusted. (Contrast this with the case of people who drive while sleepy or when under the influence of alcohol—such behavior is itself dangerous, and so a similar complaint from them will not appear to carry much weight.) In fact, the general principle of banning a certain sort of activity because a minority of people are unable to engage in it safely is one with potentially unlimited application. (Consider sport or social drinking, for example.)

An opponent of corporal punishment might reply that the above activities are either essential or very useful for our well-being,[23] but the same cannot be said of corporal punishment. It appears to be true that some parents have raised happy and well-adjusted children without using corporal punishment at all. It is not essential for anything of value. However, I believe that the resentment that may be caused to some parents as a result of being deprived of what they *believe* is an essential tool for disciplining their children is a good reason in itself for not criminalizing all corporal punishment. Occurring within the confines of the home, where it is easy to keep secret, it is a hard law to enforce, and one can even imagine that, because of the resentment factor, some parents might be encouraged to use it *more* in order to privately express their defiance of the law. I think it is better if the state merely discourages the use of all corporal punishment, and suggests to parents what alternatives might be employed in its place.

Let me hasten to add that corporal punishment of children taking the form of severe beatings should be prosecuted just as if it had been inflicted on adults. The only question concerns the less serious variety—the light slap, enough to make a child take notice, but essentially harmless and soon forgotten. This is not a *malum prohibitum*, nor is it a type of act that can be expected to cause long-term harm. In my proposed deterrent-based system, such an act would not be grounds for punishment, irrespective of whether the victim was an adult or a child. But here we face a difficulty. Slapping an adult is a form of assault. Doesn't the failure of the S-score algorithm to find it punishable draw attention to a defect in the algorithm? And if it is suitably modified to make such assaults punishable, shouldn't this include cases where the victim is a child, thus making even the mildest form of corporal punishment itself legally punishable after all?

However, there is a certain unreality about this argument. I said that I understood a 'light slap' to be one that was enough to make a child take notice, but essentially harmless and soon forgotten. In practice, I cannot think of many situations in which an adult is treated in this way. Maybe it can happen as a response to extreme rudeness from a close friend or relative. Or maybe it occurs sometimes as a joke. It wouldn't get an S-score, because it is not likely to cause long-term harm. Surely it is the user of the S-score algorithm who is in the right here, not those who (albeit understandably) want the highest standard of interpersonal behavior encoded in the criminal law. Consistently with this, we may suppose that the same actions, when directed at children, are ill-advised, but should not be subject to criminal prosecution.

NOTES

1. Though it is rather tangential to us at this point, it is interesting to note that this principle seems contrary to retributive intuitions. I argued in Sec. 1.3 that, in terms of pure deservingness, a greater temptation should involve a lessening of culpability. Yet according to Bentham's profit principle, it should attract a more severe punishment. Of course, the conflict is in no way surprising, as Bentham's principle is aimed entirely at the prevention of crime by deterrence, whereas my argument in that section was about deservingness pure and simple, to which future prevention is irrelevant.

2. It is reasonable to suppose that all other things being equal, a serious offender's probability of seriously *re*-offending diminishes as her crimes recede into the past, that as time goes on, her past behavior becomes less and less reliable as a basis for predicting her future behavior. However, we have no reliable method for determining at what point the probability becomes acceptably low. Hence I would still recommend indefinite confinement (or state-assisted suicide—see below) for the small minority of offenders that we are concerned with here.

3. A precise statement of how to determine this set in provided in the appendix.

4. It might be immoral because, given the existence of a law requiring one to drive on the right, it would be dangerous to others to drive on the left. But if so, this immorality is already dependent on the existence of the relevant law, and therefore cannot without circularity be given as the reason for making the act illegal.

5. In order to prevent the discussion from wandering too far afield, I ignore the case of harm to oneself. I am not absolutely sure, though, that I want to exclude these from the set of punishable act-types. John Stuart Mill thought we should (Mill 1910, 132), but his stance on this may not have been entirely consistent with his utilitarianism. I leave the matter open here. Note also that a full account could very well require us to consider the effects of offences on non-human animals as well.

6. An example of this would be a long-term tendency to have terrible nightmares, which do not, however, disrupt the person's ability to lead a successful life. Examples of disastrous long-term harm would be total insanity or death.

7. As the law stands in most jurisdictions, I imagine that action would be taken only if someone was actually hurt as a result. In contrast to this, the approach advocated here is not based on actual consequences, but on *expected* consequences, as explained below.

8. That is, generally known either in the population as a whole or within some group of which the offender happens to be a member (e.g. psychologists).

9. Bentham 1988, 181. His wording is that 'punishment should be adjusted in such manner to each particular offence, that for every part of the mischief there may be a motive to restrain the offender from giving birth to it.' According to my way of looking at the matter, the 'parts' of an offence distinguished by Bentham would correspond to actual offences. With this rewording understood, Bentham's point is identical to mine.

10. There is a theoretical problem here, but it need not detain us much for practical purposes. It concerns the individuation of acts through time. At what point does one act end and another begin? If a person is beaten four times, are there four distinct acts or one single act of beating someone up? Perhaps the boundary between successive acts lies at the point where the offender says to himself, 'Shall I go on with this?' (That way, there would be an appropriate link with deterrence.) But there may be many such moments in the course of a moderately complex crime (unless the criminal is extremely committed), and courts

rarely have the information necessary to identify them. Still, where there is clear evidence of such self-doubt occurring, it might be wise to set the boundary between distinct acts at that point. Otherwise, these boundaries can be based on standard ways of categorizing actions.

11. These surely have some deterrent value. They deter the sort of people who are frightened of almost *any* negative attention from the police or criminal justice system, of which, I suggest, there are very many.

12. As well as, perhaps, those who refuse to fulfil their community service orders.

13. This must depend on duration (amongst other things), which is usually a matter of speculation, since in such cases one presumes drivers typically fluctuate between states of sleepiness and wakefulness. (In Hart's case one would also have to take into account how much longer the situation *would* have lasted if it had not been interrupted by the disaster.) If the sleepy state lasts a long time (half an hour, say), how great is the chance of causing a major accident? I have no idea. My purpose is merely to consider the consequences of conceding that it *may* be quite low.

14. The new law would *not* need to declare a penalty (other than for purposes of clarification), as this could be deduced from the description of the offence plus the C-score algorithm.

15. In point of fact, if there really was the sort of moral dereliction described in my assumptions, one cannot think that there has been anything like a satisfactory response. Union Carbide's CEO, Warren Anderson, charged with manslaughter, became a 'fugitive from justice,' and has never been convicted of anything in connection with the disaster.
(See http://www.greenpeace.org/international/news/carbide-criminal-found.)

16. If this seems to create a danger of over-punishment, it should be noted that I argue below (Sec. 6.3) that all citizens should be seen as entitled to a minimum decent standard of living, in jail or out of it. So the deprivation of funds must not be so great as to plunge the individuals concerned into dire poverty. Although this does not remove the danger of over-punishment entirely, it does lessen it. If there is still thought to be a problem, the S-score algorithm will need to be applied in such a way as to allow the sentencing authority to offset any hardship created by the demands of restitution.

17. I have no problem with accepting that *Brady* was a very dangerous individual, one for whom indefinite confinement was appropriate.

18. This is because it is obvious to anyone with the intelligence to understand the case at all that it constitutes coercion. Other cases may be less clear-cut (for example, if the agent fears the thief, but it is not truly certain that she is right to do so) and it is only in relation to them that the 'slippery slope' effect that would endanger general conformity would be at all likely to occur.

19. Suppose the roles were reversed gender-wise. Suppose we were dealing with John and Andy, who are being tormented by women in ways that correspond respectively with Joanna and Anita in the original examples. Our sympathies should surely be with the men. That is why what I described as a 'feminist' bias would be wrong. On the other hand, it can be argued that in reacting the same way in both cases, we would be following *true* feminism, which requires equality of treatment between individuals, irrespective of gender.

20. More precisely, in accordance with the Revised Principle of Alternate Possibilities (see above, Sec. 2.2), the point is that she could not have had an overall intrinsic inclination not to kill her partner.

21. The word 'could' might seem obscure here, if we accept hard determinism. But discussion of the case of Joshua below should help to clarify matters.

22. However, philosophical opposition has also long existed—from Locke, for example (1693, Sec. 51-60).

23. Social drinking helps people to relax and, in some cases, take the first steps in forming valuable new relationships.

CHAPTER SIX
EFFORT AND DISTRIBUTIVE JUSTICE

6.1   Introduction

In this section we move away from the topic of punishment and into the area of positive desert, a topic that has scarcely been mentioned since Chapter One. In that chapter we thought of positive desert mainly in terms of praising or rewarding as responses to morally good actions or characters. This was to provide a parallel to the main theme of that chapter, which concerned blaming and punishing as responses to morally bad actions or characters. However, at least as far as reward (as opposed to praise) is concerned, this is not in practice what principally concerns real societies that are anything like our own, in so far as they recognize and act on positive desert. In such societies it is normally hoped that rewards will accrue mainly to those who work hard, who engage energetically in activities that the society considers 'productive.' Since it is normally the case that at least a major part of the motivation of individuals who do engage in such activities is precisely to gain the rewards (a good income and all that follows from it) which society confers upon them, it is questionable that we should view this as a truly 'moral' matter. Our societies seem mainly to reward self-interest rather than moral virtue. In considering this kind of desert, we are therefore departing from the practice laid down in the first chapter of confining our concern with desert to those cases where people are said to deserve something on the basis of *moral* appraisal. However, because the issue of effort and hard work is so closely linked to that of distributive justice and the latter *is* a moral matter, I think it is right that I should deal with it in this book.

First, we need to clarify exactly what is involved in attaching positive desert to hard work. Is it the achievement that is important or the effort made or a combination of both? If we follow the internalist view defended in the first chapter, the answer is clear. It must be the effort and the effort alone. For no-one can legitimately receive any credit for what is not strictly due to him, and any actual achievement, to the extent that it depends on more than the agent's own efforts (e.g., on good luck or the help of others) is not strictly due to him and so should not get him any extra credit. Furthermore, it is not every aspect of effort-making that is relevant. The contraction of muscles depends on some factors (such as a healthy physique) that are to a large extent beyond the agent's control. It is only the *mental* aspect of effort which could be said to be strictly within the agent's control (determinism aside) and so could be said to ground desert—if anything does. So the question I want to pose is this: is it in fact true that people who make a *mental effort* to engage in 'productive' work deserve to be rewarded for doing so? As might be expected, my answer is no, and my principal reasons mirror those developed in relation to negative desert:

- Because people's mental efforts (as opposed to their overt actions) are to a large extent hidden from us, it is very hard for us to assess them.

- Even if we can know people's mental efforts on specific occasions, we face the problem that any given reward might represent 'superfluous happiness,' the positive analogue of superfluous suffering. In other words, the recipient might already have been sufficiently rewarded by past happiness (or might be going to receive an adequate measure of happiness in the future). To assess this would require detailed information about the person's past (and even future) life that we rarely have in practice. Of course, this problem is not as serious as that of superfluous suffering, as an 'excess' of happiness, unlike an excess of suffering, is not an intrinsically bad thing. But it is of *some* concern. Those who want to reward effort are usually concerned with fairness, and if some people are receiving superfluous happiness in the sense explained, that seems to be unfair on those who get no more than the 'correct' amount.

- In any case, hard determinism robs people of the kind of responsibility for their mental efforts that would make it reasonable to say that they deserve rewards for them.

Although I believe all these points have considerable force, I do not want to ground my critique of effort-based positive desert on them alone, particularly in view of their controversial character. I want to engage with a discussion that more frequently arises in relation to positive desert and distributive justice. This concerns John Rawls' claim that talented individuals do not deserve the goods that they obtain from society through the use of their talents.

6.2 Sher versus Rawls

Rawls has famously argued that people who achieve success through the exercise of their native talents do not thereby deserve any rewards that they might obtain through doing so (Rawls 1999, 89). His argument for this is that such people have done nothing to create their native talents and so can receive no credit for them or for the productive work made possible by them. If we all had equal talents or abilities, we would all be starting on a level playing field, as it were, and perhaps some of us could deserve rewards on the basis of the better use that we put these abilities to. But since we clearly have different native abilities and are not responsible for whatever native gifts we do have, it would be unfair for any of us to enjoy extra benefit from them, as compared with others who have inferior talents. Hence we may be said not to deserve such extra benefit.

Sher (amongst many others) has challenged Rawls's argument (Sher 1987, 22-36). He suggests that there is one ability in particular that may not be equally distributed, and that is the very ability that I am treating as crucial here: the ability to make an effort. He suggests that for all we know, different people might have exactly the same level of ability to make an effort. General deterministic arguments aside, this would make it plausible to suppose that some people deserve rewards for their greater use of this ability, as compared with others who use it less.

But *is* effort-making ability equally distributed? Sher rightly points out that the fact that people differ so greatly in the amount of effort they *do* make does not prove that they have different levels of ability in effort-making. For this difference in people's performance can easily be explained by the fact that people are often inclined not to *make* the efforts necessary to achieve various goals, because, for example, they do not consider these goals to be *worth* the effort required, or because they have conflicting goals that override them. But Sher seems to assume that the onus of proof here lies on those who reject the thesis of equal effort-making ability. This does not seem to me correct. If we all had an equal ability to make an effort, then this would, as far as we know, be the *only* ability that human beings had the same amount of. Humans differ in their levels of ability with respect to any other activity you may care to think of, from walking along a tightrope to solving quadratic equations. It would be very surprising if there was an exception to this rule. There is also a more abstract argument that can be used against the equal ability thesis, as long as it is accepted that all abilities human beings have are ultimately biologically or physically based. It is simply this: owing to genetic and environmental variation, it is practically impossible, on this premise, for any ability to fail to show some variation amongst a (sufficiently large) population.

However, I do not think this is the end of the story. For what I have just argued shows at most that *if* there is such a thing as effort-making ability—in the sense of a specific sort of faculty—it is almost certainly unequally distributed. But I also think we should seriously doubt that there is such a thing, for reasons that I shall now explain.

What exactly is it to make an effort? If effort is needed to do something, this implies the existence of some desire not to do it. But of course this cannot be just any sort of desire. It has to be a desire rooted in torpor or laziness. To make an effort to do something, then, is to succeed in overcoming a contrary desire that is rooted in torpor or laziness.

It does seem to be the case that there exists a generic attribute called laziness. People may have this attribute as a permanent part of their personality, or (and I think more frequently) they may go through periods of laziness. During such a period, a person may have good reasons, even in her own terms, for doing certain things, but she cannot seem to muster the energy to do them (and there is no medical reason for this—for example, M.E.). The attribute is *generic* because it is not tied to any particular activity that the person has a reason to do. Rather, it inhibits a range of such activities (although of course there are usually *some* things that even a lazy person will like to do).

One might think that if there is such a thing as generic laziness, then there must be such a thing as a generic effort-making ability that could overcome it. But this does not follow, and indeed, it is very plausible to suppose that there is no such thing. To clarify this, let us first remind ourselves that our concern here is with mental effort, not physical effort. No-one would deny that all tasks require physical effort. Muscles need to be contracted to engender the required bodily movements. (An exception would be 'tasks' that simply involve thinking about something.) But it is common for people to think that in addition to the physical effort, one needs a kind of mental 'push,' often called 'will power' or 'volition.' And it is natural to suppose that the stronger the disinclination, the stronger the mental 'push' needed to overcome it.

William James takes issue with this. Here is what he has to say about how we manage to get out of a warm bed on a cold day:

> If I may generalize from my own experience, we more often than not get up without any struggle or decision at all. We suddenly find that we *have* got up. A fortunate lapse of consciousness occurs; we forget both the warmth and the cold; we fall into some reverie connected with the day's life, in the course of which the idea flashes across us, "Hollo! I must lie here no longer"—an idea which at that lucky instant awakens no contradictory or paralyzing suggestions, and consequently produces immediately its appropriate motor effects. (James 1890, 524)

Of course, not all our decisions are made in this way, and James considers other sorts of examples, including cases where real deliberation is needed. But always he is able to sustain the notion that what mentally precedes the voluntary action is some kind of *idea*, which is able to bring about the required motor effects. A distinct sort of psychic event—a volition—is neither evident to introspection, nor needed by a sound psychological theory of what is going on.

But if this is correct, then lazy people do not fail to do things for want of mental effort or will power. They fail to do them because, at the crucial times, they do not have the ideas that are needed to make them act. But this failing would seem to indicate, if anything, a deficiency in intelligence—for which people are not usually thought blameworthy— rather than a failure to make use of a specific sort of faculty which we all have, whether in equal or unequal amounts.

If I am right, there is no specific phenomenon of making a mental effort,[1] and there is therefore no generic effort-making *ability*. In that case, Sher is wrong to suppose that there are people who are more deserving of benefits than others because they make better use of this ability than those others, and Rawls' argument against such desert remains untouched, at any rate by this line of thinking.

6.3   Distributive justice

In Chapter Three I abandoned desert as a basis for justified punishment. This made it necessary to develop an alternative justification in the following two chapters. My rejection of desert as the basis for the distribution of society's benefits similarly creates an obligation on my part to indicate, at least in a rough way, an alternative, more reasonable, basis for just distribution. However, as we shall see, my suggestions will be more derivative than those that I have made with regard to punishment, as I believe the essential work has already been done by another philosopher. (Hence the brevity of this chapter as compared with its two predecessors.)

What are the main alternatives? In his *Anarchy, State and Utopia*, Robert Nozick advocates a system in which people acquire goods according to principles of just acquisition that are purely 'historical' in nature (Nozick 2001, 153). Goods are considered to be acquired justly provided that they are either acquired directly from 'nature,' subject to a proviso (derived from Locke) that there must be 'as much and as good' left over for others *or* from another person (who already holds them justly) by some form of voluntary agreement (e.g., sale, gift etc.). The resulting system is a very pure form of market economy. There is no attempt to distribute goods according to desert or indeed according to any other higher moral principle such as equality. In fact, it is misleading, according to Nozick, to talk of 'distribution' of goods in the first place. No central agency organizes the acquisition of goods by individuals (Nozick 2001, 149). It happens either by original acquisition or by voluntary transfer involving only the individuals concerned. Nozick believes such a system is more just than any other, since its voluntary aspect involves respecting people's rights. Other proposed systems, such as those involving a central distributing agency, will be coercive and hence not respectful of people's rights.

However, as many critics have pointed out, Nozick's system has aspects which few would regard as morally acceptable. (See, for example, La Follette 1978 and Singer 1978.) Nozick would forbid any taxation aimed at relieving the plight of desperately poor people, because of its coercive character. Yet it seems a much higher moral priority to relieve the plight of desperately poor people than to respect the 'right' of a wealthy entrepreneur not to be deprived of a relatively small amount of money.

Let us now consider the position of Nozick's great rival, John Rawls, one of whose important observations has already been discussed and defended earlier in this chapter. We have also seen (in Section 4.4) that Rawls believes the justice of institutions to be logically prior to the issue of what people deserve. This entails that, although Rawls does not reject the concept of desert, he cannot use it to determine what would make for just institutions. So what does determine this, according to him? His answer is complex, but can be roughly summarized as follows. Firstly, there is a principle of liberty, which requires that institutions be designed so as to guarantee the greatest possible freedom for each citizen compatible with the same freedom for others. Secondly, there is the famous *difference principle*, which requires that any inequality in the distribution of so-called primary goods (i.e., those goods—such as food and shelter—which every rational person wants) must be such as to result in an increase in the well-being of the worst off in society. For example, the extra benefits that the talented receive through the use of their talents in a generally open market might be justified, not because they deserve those extra benefits, but rather by virtue of the fact that the prospect of gaining them creates an incentive for them to work harder, without which they would not produce as much wealth, and this would be detrimental even to the worst off (assuming that the latter receive some of the benefit, perhaps through lower prices). Only without some such justification can inequalities between people in their possession of primary goods be regarded as morally acceptable, in Rawls' view (1999, 52-6).

Rawls has had numerous critics. One particularly interesting criticism comes from Gerald Cohen (1992). Cohen argues that there is a tension between two stances that might be adopted by the talented. On the one hand, they might acknowledge the moral importance of improving the worst off in society, advocating incentives for this purpose. On the other hand, they may themselves demand incentives to work harder. The reason that these stances are in tension with one another is that if the talented decided to work harder *without* incentives, there would be even more wealth available from which to draw benefits to the worst off. The way to overcome this tension, according to Cohen, is for the talented to agree to work harder *without* receiving incentives for doing so. In this way the moral imperative to help the worst off will be *maximally* satisfied.

But Cohen's argument is flawed. He assumes that those advocating incentives on broadly Rawlsian or egalitarian grounds and those demanding to have them are the same people. But this may not be so. For example, a philosophy professor can consistently (a) hold that talented people in general need to be given incentives for the sake of the worst off, because otherwise they will not produce the needed extra wealth and (b) refuse any extra income intended as an incentive for *her*. She can take both stances because she believes that others will not be so conscientious as to adopt stance (b), as she has done. On the other hand, Cohen may have a good *ad hominem* point, for it is likely that a number of Rawlsian philosophy professors, and others who advocate incentives to help the worst off, do not refuse such incentives for themselves. Still, it remains true that Cohen has not, through this line of thought, revealed any *logical* inconsistency in the Rawlsian philosopher's position on this point.

However, I would reject Rawls' Difference Principle for another reason. The principle requires that any inequality must benefit the worst off, irrespective of the latter's absolute level of well-being. But consider a scenario in which even the worst off are very well off indeed. There may not be many societies in which this is true, but it is a theoretical possibility, and a general principle of justice needs to take account of it. The problem is that it is very implausible to suppose that there is any moral requirement for inequalities to benefit the worst off when the latter are already very comfortably off anyway. True, it is theoretically possible for there to be wide disparities of well-being even when the lowest are, in absolute terms, at a very high level, and these disparities might still be thought unfair if they did not result in any improvement for the worst off. But why? If the worst off are actually very well off, if they have all the necessities of life and much more besides, why should it be a matter of concern that others are even better off? It is possible that the worst off might envy those people. Indeed, this is quite likely, as it is known that envy can be sparked off by large disparities in wealth even when the lowest are doing quite well. But if these feelings of envy are only mild, then it is far from clear that removing them is a high priority.[2] If, on the other hand, they are very strong, then their existence would be incompatible with the hypothesis that the worst off are at a high absolute level of well-being and so would not be relevant to the argument.

The same objection can be made against a more familiar theory of just distribution: *egalitarianism*, which, in the context of the present discussion, maintains that all people—or all citizens of a given state—should enjoy (roughly) equal levels of well-being.[3] The difference between this view and Rawls' is that the latter permits certain inequalities, whereas the former bans all of them. But of course this difference will not protect the egalitarian from the force of the above objection. For there seems to be no intrinsic value in having greater equality *per se* when even the worst off are already very comfortably off.

We thus need something better than both Rawlsian justice and egalitarianism. Ted Honderich has suggested a promising approach. Instead of advocating equality of well-being, he advocates a *Principle of Humanity*, which, in broad terms, imposes on each of us—but more particularly on the state—an obligation to try to 'keep people out of bad lives' (Honderich 2006, 208). The advantage of this approach is that it focuses on what seems to matter—people's absolute levels of well-being—and so does not compel us to assist people who are well off in absolute terms when they happen to be worse off than others.[4] I believe Honderich's general approach is the best hope at the present time for a satisfactory theory of distributive justice.[5] We should also note, by the way, that it is a form of utilitarianism—not, it is true, in Honderich's own usage of the term (it is not aggregative), but certainly in my broader (and more usual) sense.

An important clarification is required here. I have argued that any fundamental principle of distributive justice should make no reference to desert based on effort. But it should not be inferred from this that all uses of the word 'deserve' should be expunged from the discussion of this issue. We might say, for example, that nurses deserve to be paid more. This is legitimate, provided our grounds for saying so are of the right sort. If we say this because we think that nurses freely choose to make big efforts on behalf of their patients, and thus deserve to be rewarded with better pay, then this, according to my arguments, would be incorrect. However, our grounds might be of a different sort. We might say instead that the working lives of nurses contain a lot of drudgery, and hence a significant amount of irritation and discomfort, a lot more than in many other jobs. We might then think that they ought to have the income—and the time—to enable them to engage in activities that are more relaxing and enjoyable in order to produce a better balance in their lives between what they enjoy doing and what they have to do but dislike doing. If this is what we mean when we say that nurses deserve to be paid more, we are not appealing to the kind of desert based on effort that I have targeted here, but to a different and, in my view, more defensible kind (and, I should add, one compatible with a broadly conceived utilitarianism).[6]

One final thread needs to be tied up, and it runs between the topics of distributive justice and punishment. In Chapter Three our discussion of Corlett's views raised a problem concerning the living conditions of prisoners. It was pointed out that my utilitarian approach seemed to leave us with no reason for spending money on keeping these conditions bearable, instead of using the same money for other 'worthy' causes. I think we can see now how we might resolve this problem. The Principle of Humanity, when seriously implemented, would require the provision by the state of a minimum income, at least enough to afford basic necessities. And there is no reason why criminals serving time should be an exception. Indeed, we have, if anything, *more* reason to insist on this for prisoners than for others, for the following reason. When the state provides income to free citizens, we know that some of them will use it in ways contrary to the aim of securing a decent level of well-being for them and their families (e.g. buying excessive amounts of alcohol). When, in contrast, we are dealing with prisoners receiving goods from the state, we can prevent this, or at least minimize it.

NOTES

1. Several other writers besides James have taken this view. A classic critique is Ryle 1949, 61-80.

2. Perhaps an increase in certain intellectual and cultural goods that not all citizens are able to benefit from outweighs the minor badness of the fact that those who miss out feel envious.

3. There are other versions of egalitarianism, which require equality in other things e.g. equality of opportunity, equality of income etc. These are, however, rather superficial forms of egalitarianism. The keen egalitarian will take note of the fact that there can be equality with respect to these other things even when people enjoy widely different levels of well-being. Intuitively, it is surely well-being that really matters.

4. I do not mean to suggest that we must attach *no* importance to relative levels of well-being. There can be reasons, having to do with envy (mentioned above) and the danger of inter-class conflict, for addressing it, but they are instrumental reasons—we need not worry about relative well-being in and of itself.

5. It is also very abstract and politically neutral (at least as I understand it). Accepting it does not commit us to any particular form of social or economic organization. If, for example, a market economy would be best at keeping people out of bad lives, then the principle would endorse it.

6. Notice the similarity of the nurse example to Fred Feldman's case of Jim, mentioned in Section 1.2. Both involve types of desert unrelated to any specific merits of the individual concerned.

CHAPTER SEVEN
MORALITY AND BLAME

7.1 Hostility to wrongdoers

In this chapter I adopt a major change of perspective. I have been largely concerned up until now with the 'public' matters of state punishment and distributive justice. Now it is time to look at the 'private' sphere of personal morality. Just as we asked how the state should respond to wrongdoing without recourse to the idea of desert, we now ask how each of us, as moral agents, should respond to the wrongdoing of other moral agents (and our own) under the same restriction.

As far as the state is concerned, we saw that absence of desert did not entail that a punitive response to wrongdoing was always inappropriate, and indeed, we found that such a response is justified at least when the wrongdoing is serous. The parallel line in relation to the private moral sphere would involve arguing that even though individuals who do immoral things that are not covered by the state punishment system may not *deserve* criticism, blame or other harsh reactions, such responses are nevertheless sometimes justified in this sphere also. Can such an argument be successfully made?

One way of doing this might be to suppose that there is a conceptual link between morality and hostility to wrongdoing of a sort that would make it logically impossible to have the former without the latter. Some writers have taken this line. For example, Peter French, many of whose views about punishment we have already encountered, follows J.L Mackie (1985, 214) in arguing that the very concept of morality entails an obligation to respond with hostility to acts of wrongdoing. He urges this point very strongly:

> Getting even . . . is noneliminable from a moral system. (French 2001, 97)

More fully:

> Condonation of wrongful actions, of evil, is morally impermissible. It is no better than collusion. My claim then is that if we have a concept of moral wrong at all, it includes the notion that whatever is morally wrong must be met with an antagonistic response from the members of the moral community. (French 2001, 97)

He describes the need for hostility in response to wrongdoing as 'one of the primary foundations of morality . . . settled in passions, attitudes, emotions and sentiments, not in reason' (French 2001, 97).

Is this correct? Let us first take a look at the precise import of the phrase 'hostility to wrongdoing' and others like them. While it is true that we habitually use such phrases, I believe that they can be misleading. We cannot, strictly speaking, be hostile to an act. We can think an act bad or have a negative attitude towards it, but that is not quite the same thing as being hostile to it. When we talk about being hostile to an act, the hostility we refer to is really directed towards the act's perpetrator. This is not just a verbal quibble. When a philosopher says that morality necessitates being hostile to acts of wrongdoing, we may take him to be saying merely that if you adopt a moral stance you must of necessity think that certain sorts of acts are bad or have a negative attitude to such acts. This would be hard to dispute. But because of the way we normally use the word 'hostile,' there is an implication smuggled in that if we take morality seriously, we must necessarily think badly of certain sorts of *people*. We are thus already on the way to a retributive way of looking at things, through what is in effect a kind of semantic sleight of hand (though it may be unconscious on the part of those using it).

So the real question we must address is this. Is it the case that someone who adopts the moral stance must, simply in virtue of doing so, have hostile attitudes towards certain sorts of people? Traditional Christian morality includes the adage 'Love the sinner, but hate the sin,' which seems to contradict this—indeed, it supports the opposite idea that true morality requires forbearance and forgiveness, rather than hostility. At this point, though, I only wish to argue for the weaker claim that morality does not at any rate necessitate hostility towards anyone. For this purpose, I shall present a thought experiment.

Consider a community of human-like beings called the *doves*. The doves have certain rules or principles that govern their lives. These rules determine how they are supposed to treat one another, and are very similar to the core moral rules of most human societies: do not tell lies, do not steal, do not harm or injure others and so on. However, there is one big difference between the doves and us in relation to such rules. Though doves occasionally violate these rules, no dove ever disparages another dove for doing so. In fact, in such situations, the errant dove is never subjected to a negative response of any kind. On the other hand, doves do often point out the bad aspects of certain *acts*, in particular their violation of one or more of the rules. But when they do so in the presence of other doves who have violated these rules, the latter, far from feeling ashamed or distressed, welcome these remarks as helpful reminders of ways in which they might improve their conduct in future. Another feature of the social life of doves is their tendency to praise those who commit very few violations of the rules, particularly in the face of great temptation.

Now, based on the above description, isn't it reasonable to say that the doves have a moral code? There seems to be so much in common between what

I specified about them and what is implied by the term 'moral code' as it is normally understood in relation to human societies as to make the refusal to apply this term to the doves' way of life arbitrary and unwarranted. More specifically: the doves have rules of conduct whose content is very similar to our moral rules; they often think it worthwhile to point out other doves' violations of these rules; and they value conformity to the rules to the extent of praising those doves who are particularly good at following them. And yet doves never disparage or blame one another for violating their rules. Therefore, *pace* Mackie and French, the concept of morality or a moral code does not necessitate hostility to wrongdoers.

Now of course, it is not likely that we human beings could be exactly like the doves. In fact it may be impossible in a sort of biological sense. We have already seen Mackie's plausible argument that hostility to wrongdoers has a biological origin. In fact, my recognition that the doves' characteristics might be incompatible with being fully human was registered by my description of them as 'human-*like*.' But why should morality be confined to humans? I know of no careful account of morality which ties it exclusively to our own species. Of course, most writers think that being a moral being carries with it certain characteristics, such as the capacity for rational thought, which humans possess. But this does not by any means entail that morality is confined to humans, since, in principle at least, these characteristics could be possessed by other beings. So even if the doves are not human, this does not in itself prevent them from being moral. Indeed, I can see no reason why we should deny them this attribute.

But this may not be the end of the matter. Perhaps French and his allies could advance a weaker, but more plausible, thesis that would prove their point. They could maintain that the *combination* of a moral code with a nature such as we humans have necessarily entails hostility towards moral wrongdoers. The thinking behind this might be that acceptance of certain moral rules, combined with a tendency to hostile reactions towards those who act differently from the way we would like them to act (which is arguably an element of 'human nature') will necessarily entail a tendency to react to *moral* wrongdoers with condemnation and hostility. This might be considered as tight a connection between morality and hostility to moral wrongdoers as one could reasonably wish for. (It scarcely seems to matter that the argument would have to be restricted to human beings and relevantly similar creatures.) But does the alleged entailment actually obtain?

The problem is not so much that the entailment is straightforwardly false as that it skates over too much complexity. For there is a whole range of degrees of 'reactivity' that different morally conscientious individuals can manifest towards morally incorrect behavior, from a calm and resigned sadness to a furious righteous anger. Biological generalizations about human nature may determine shared human tendencies, but they do not determine the particular reactive propensities of individuals in specific sorts of situations.

We cannot get much further with this issue through the mere examination of concepts. What we need is some substantive reason for thinking certain kinds of emotional reactions to wrongdoers *preferable* to others. The most obvious candidates (at least from the perspective of this book) are utilitarian or consequentialist reasons. It may be argued that certain sorts of reactions are to be preferred because they are the ones most conducive to human well-being. French's attitude to consequences is, as we have seen, somewhat ambivalent. But surely we can agree at least that it is important to take into account the likely consequences of different kinds of reactive attitudes. But when we do so, the situation revealed is not a straightforward one. It is undoubtedly true that hostility and anger towards wrongdoers is sometimes conducive to good consequences. This is perhaps most obvious in the context of child-rearing. A parent may castigate an errant child, and to do this is to show a kind of fleeting hostility towards the child. This is not necessarily feigned hostility. For a moment, the parent may well feel hateful towards her child. Fortunately, this does not normally undermine the deep bond between parent and child, because of its transient nature. And it may be justified if the result is (or could reasonably be expected to be) that the child avoids the relevant sort of wrongdoing in future.

But is hostility similarly effective in relation to adult wrongdoers? Could it work as a deterrent to wrongdoing in the same way that state punishment often does? Almost certainly. But how often does it happen? That is a harder question to answer. If A is hostile to B because B did X, how B reacts to this depends very much on how she perceives A. If she has respect for A, it is quite likely that the deterrent effect will occur. If she is indifferent to A, it will not. And if she is herself hostile to A, this may make repeated wrongdoing on her part *more* likely, rather than less so. In general, it is difficult to say whether deterrence happens often enough to make a significant contribution to diminishing the frequency of morally unacceptable behavior. Consider the sort of person who repeatedly engages in acts of bullying others in ways that they find quite unpleasant, but not serious enough for state action by the criminal justice system. How should third parties react to such a person if their aim is to deter, not just the culprit himself, but others who might be disposed to behave in similar ways? How much do such people take the reactions of the 'moral community' into account? Doubtless this varies from one individual to another, and the overall effect is hard to establish. It is thus difficult to make any definite recommendation on consequentialist grounds. My tentative suggestion is that when such matters arise, one does best to avoid acts of hostility, such as shunning, emotional coldness or insults—which are of roughly the same sort as those one wishes to discourage, since this, by setting a better example, may well be more effective in upholding morality.

Closely associated with the subject of blame is that of guilt. Indeed, guilt is presumably a special case of blame, in which one blames oneself. These days, popular psychology and self-help manuals tend to counsel against having guilt feelings. The reader will not be surprised to learn that, on the whole, I agree with this stance. It is true that guilt can on occasion inhibit people from doing bad things. For example, a person might well say to herself (or have it said to her by someone else): 'Remember how guilty you felt last time you got so drunk—you don't want to feel like that again, do you?' and avoid drunkenness as a result. Here the prospect of blaming oneself acts as a kind of deterrent, just as blaming others may do. But it has its dangers. Most importantly, it may fail to have the deterrent effect, even if it is very intense. In such cases it produces a great deal of pointless unhappiness, even, on occasion, to the point of clinical depression. Note that if a person feels guilty as a result of having acted badly, this is usually associated with some degree of morally-rooted disinclination to perform the relevant sort of act, a disinclination that will usually (though not always[1]) have existed before the given occasion of wrongdoing, but was not strong enough to override competing temptations. This being so, it seems better on the whole for those seeking improvements in the person's behavior to try to build on this by providing additional motives—e.g., the thought of securing praise or reward. On balance, I think it is rarely a wise thing to encourage guilt—one may intensify pain with no overriding improvement in the agent's behavior.

7.2　Sher on blame

No treatment of this subject would be complete without a consideration of the argument propounded by George Sher in his book *In Praise of Blame* (Sher 2006) to the conclusion that blame is an essential constituent of morality, that the latter would be inconceivable without it.

Sher maintains that the concept of blame has two distinct components: a belief that someone has behaved badly or has a bad character *plus* something else. It is specifying the nature of the 'something else' which creates most of the difficulty, and much of Sher's book is devoted to grappling with this problem.

Before providing his own analysis of blame, Sher presents three existing alternative views and finds fault with all of them. The first is a proposal 'favored by some utilitarians . . . that what we are doing when we blame someone is expressing our disapproval of his behavior or character in a way that we hope will change it' (Sher 2006, 13; see also 71-4). He rejects this theory on the grounds that blame does not always have to be overtly expressed, but can be just a private thought (Sher 2006, 74). The second theory, of which Michael Zimmerman is an exponent (1988, 38-9), is that 'what blaming someone adds to believing that he has acted badly or is a bad person is some sort of further belief—for example, that his misbehavior has somehow stained his "moral record" or reduced his "moral balance"' (Sher 2006, 13; see also 75-8). This view is rejected on the grounds that its advocates cannot explain why we should take any interest in people's 'moral balance' over and above our interest in the fact that they have acted badly (Sher 2006, 78). The final theory considered by Sher is that to blame someone is to react to her with some negative emotion such as anger or hostility.[2] He rejects this view on the grounds that its defenders cannot give a credible explanation of why some people are *worthy* of blame. Acting badly or having a bad character cannot be enough in itself—we are not entitled to be angry with just anyone of whom this is true (Sher 2006, 87).

The theory of blame subsequently offered by Sher himself to replace these inadequate views (and I agree that they *are* inadequate) is that to blame someone is to believe that she has done something wrong or that she has a bad character plus also to have the desire or wish that she not have done this wrong thing or that she not have this bad character (Sher 2006, 14; see also 93-114). This account has such merits as the fact that it evidently allows blame to be a purely private matter (for the desire referred to need not be expressed), and the fact that it explains why when one blames another one has certain dispositions, namely: to feel anger or hostility to that person, to reproach or reprimand her, or (when the person blamed is oneself) to apologize for what one has done. (But notice that unlike in the third of the existing theories considered by Sher, blame is not *identified* with such dispositions.)

Sher moves on from the presentation and defense of this analysis to consider the question of why those who act badly or have a bad character might be considered *worthy* of blame (Sher 2006, 115-138). His answer is that this follows from the very nature of morality, more specifically from certain formal features which, it is agreed by almost everyone, moral principles must possess. They must be *practical* (primarily for guiding action), *universal* (applying to everyone), *omnitemporal* (applying at all times), *overriding* (having priority over virtually every other consideration) and *inescapable* (such that no-one can opt out of their requirements). The practicality of moral principles entails that if one accepts a moral principle one must have at least some desire to do what it says. Their universality and omnitemporality respectively entail that this desire must apply to others besides oneself, and must extend beyond the present to the past and future. Finally, their overridingness and inescapability together entail that this desire must have the sort of strength that would be needed to give rise to a disposition to feel anger and hostility.

As well as showing why it is appropriate to blame those who have done wrong or who have a bad character, Sher also thinks that this theory explains why such people *deserve* blame, since, he argues, to make such a desert claim *is* just to state that such blame would be appropriate (Sher 2006, 131).

I turn now to the evaluation of Sher's theory.[3] I accept that *if* his analysis of blame is correct, this entails that morality generally renders blame appropriate for wrongdoers, and roughly for the reasons explained by Sher. However, I want to establish the following:

(i) Sher has not in fact succeeded in explaining why blame, understood in terms of his analysis, can be *deserved*.
(ii) Sher's analysis of blame is in any case incomplete in a way that casts additional doubt on the claim that wrongdoers generally deserve blame.

First, to explain why, even if we accept Sher's analysis of blame, we should reject his account of why people deserve blame, understood in his sense. The reason for this has to do with a certain conceptual point about desert which we noted as early as Section 1.4, namely, that whenever a person negatively deserves something, what she deserves (in the strictest moral sense) must be something that she experiences as bad or unpleasant. It is clear that Sher is working with a rather more anemic version of desert, whereby to say that someone deserves something (positive or negative) means little more than that it would be appropriate for her to receive it. But as a matter of conceptual necessity, this is not enough for desert. It also needs the fact that the deserving person would experience what she deserves as pleasant (in the case of positive desert) or as unpleasant (in the case of negative desert). Nothing in Sher's analysis of blame explains why a person for whom blame was, according to that analysis, appropriate ought to be treated in a way that she would find unpleasant. For being the subject of a belief that one has acted badly plus a desire that one not have acted in this way is not an intrinsically unpleasant thing. True, Sher's account does readily explain why someone might deserve blame in *his* sense of the word. For it is indeed the case that if someone has done something bad, thus flouting or ignoring some requirement of morality, it would be appropriate both to believe that this is the case and to wish that she had not done it. But that fact is not sufficient to establish that she deserves blame in the full sense of (negative) desert, requiring treatment that she would find unpleasant.

Now to establish my second point, which is that Sher's analysis of blame is incomplete. To make the point with sufficient care, I need to distinguish between what I shall call *third person* and *second person* blame. Third person blame is expressed when A says sincerely that she blames B for something, but has no particular intention that B know this. In contrast, second person blame is expressed when A says that she blames B with precisely this intention. It is expressed by using 'I blame you for . . .' and similar phrases.[4] There is also of course *first person* blame, in which one blames oneself, and which usually takes the form of guilt feelings.

Second person blame appears essential to our overall concept of blame, and so any satisfactory analysis of blame must deal successfully with it. Now, in this connection, it is important to note that to express second person blame to someone is not merely to report one's own attitudes to her or to what she has done. If you sincerely say to someone 'I blame you for X,' then you will necessarily be doing something that she is likely to find unwelcome. Those who are learning the use of the word in its second person occurrence have to realize this, on pain of not fully grasping what is involved in this speech-act. Notice that this characterization does not require a blamer to *intend* that the blamee be distressed. That need not be my aim in blaming you for something, but, in doing so, I must believe that there is some likelihood[5] that you will find it unwelcome.

We need not concern ourselves with the psychological or sociological origins of the speech-act of expressing second person blame. No doubt they have something to do with the survival value of a certain kind of social control (as we saw in Mackie's theory of the biological origins of retributive feelings, discussed in Section 3.2). The important point for us here is that second person blame exists and seems to form an essential part of our entire notion of blaming. In particular, an understanding of second person blame seems essential to a correct account of third person blame. For if A blames B in the third person sense for doing X, then this seems to mean—at a minimum—that A believes that B did

X in such a way as to satisfy standard criteria for moral responsibility and that because of this, according to conventional moral precepts, one would be justified in expressing second person blame to B. Again, first person blame can be regarded as equivalent to either third or second person blame, with the special feature that the person blamed is identical to the person who is blaming. In other words, one expresses first person blame either by saying to another that one blames oneself (third person) or (perhaps less often) by saying to oneself something along the lines of 'I blame you' (second person).

So blame is a more complex matter than even Sher's sophisticated analysis allows for—and in a way that brings into question his belief (which he is far from alone in holding) that wrongdoers generally deserve blame. Given the stronger conception of blame that I have advocated here, as opposed to Sher's weaker concept, it still needs explaining why this would be the case—in particular why wrongdoers would ever deserve to be the recipients of *second person* blame, i.e., to be addressed in a way that they would be likely to find unwelcome.

The defect that I have identified in Sher's analysis of blame is no trivial matter, particularly given one of the major aims announced in his book, which is to try to establish that some people deserve blame without having to address the complex issue of determinism and its implications for moral responsibility. If I am right, Sher only manages to avoid getting stuck in this quagmire by missing out the very element in the nature of blame that makes moral responsibility and determinism relevant—its necessary connection with the idea of wrongdoers' being treated in ways that they find unwelcome. (If determinism is true, how can anyone ever deserve to have an unwelcome feeling?) Bring that element back in—as, I have argued, we are conceptually obliged to do—and determinism is seen to be as threatening as ever to our established practices of blame and of holding people morally responsible for their actions.

It may aid our understanding of these matters if we return for a moment to the doves. It will be recalled that, although doves often point out to one another violations of their rules of conduct, they never do so in a disparaging or hostile way. Do doves ever *blame* one another? It seems to me that they do in Sher's sense of the word. For that kind of blame requires only a belief that another has done something bad or has a bad character plus the desire that this person not have done this bad thing or have this bad character, which is something that is often true of the doves. But do doves blame each other in what I have identified as the true and complete sense of blaming, requiring recognition of the speech-act of expressing second-person blame, understood according to my proposed analysis? Since the latter requires a willingness to let another person feel discomfort or distress, and since the doves do not *disparage* each other when they point out each other's failings, it is clear that they do not in fact blame one another in this sense. In fact, we could reverse this point and use the example of the doves as evidence for the incompleteness of Sher's analysis. Intuitively, we are not prepared to say that doves ever blame one another, and a good explanation of this is precisely their lack of willingness to inflict distress or discomfort on others when pointing out their failings, i.e., to adopt a state of mind necessary for sincere second person blame. And the example of the doves can also be used to undermine another of Sher's theses. For although it is true that most of us will not want to say that doves ever blame one another, I believe (as indicated earlier) that most of us will want to say that they do have a kind of morality, thus supporting my contention that morality does not necessitate blame. Notice that we can also say that having a morality does not require a community even to have a *concept* of blame. But in that case, having a morality does not require having the concept of *deserving* blame either.

I want to end this chapter with a clarification concerning the relationship between my views and those of George Sher. Up to now, the impression may have been created that we are very far apart on the question of blame. However, at least where practical ethics is concerned, the difference is not as great as it appears. The reason for this is as follows. Sher maintains, as we have seen, that a logically necessary condition for blame is the presence of a belief that someone has acted badly or has a bad character plus a desire that she not have acted thus or not have such a character. Such a belief-desire pair tends to give rise to certain dispositions such as anger or hostility. But Sher is undecided about whether these dispositions are themselves also logically necessary for blame. My own view, which I defended above, is that the belief-desire pair is not sufficient. But in any case, Sher recognizes the possibility of a kind of 'stripped down' blame, which requires *only* the belief-desire pair, not the dispositions normally associated with them. He then briefly addresses the question of whether it would be possible for human beings to make do with just this stripped down version. He is not sure of the answer to this question, but suggests that 'it may be possible to improve the quality of our social relations by lowering the condemnatory volume and compensating for any resulting diminution of social control in other ways' (Sher 2006, 138). I thoroughly agree.

NOTES

1. An agent might become guilty about having done X as a result of *subsequently* learning that X was a bad thing to do.

2. Sher 2006, 13; see also 78-91. Strawson (1974, 1-25) is mentioned as one of the main sources for this view.

3. I focus entirely on blame for bad acts, ignoring bad characters. This is because I do not want to get embroiled here in the discussion of whether it is ever right to blame a person for her bad character. (Of course, whether or not it is ever right, I would maintain that it is never deserved.)

4. There are in fact a great variety of ways of expressing second person blame. They do not all use the word 'blame' or any synonym of it. If my wife says to me 'You didn't do the washing up' in a certain tone of voice, this can be an expression of second person blame.

5. By this I mean a likelihood *all other things being equal.* In some cases I might know that the blamee is particularly thick-skinned and will feel no distress.

CHAPTER EIGHT
CONCLUSION:
DESERT SKEPTICS IN A VENGEFUL WORLD

Here is a summary of the argument of this book. In Chapter One I drew attention to some problems in applying the concept of desert based on moral appraisal, problems which, I argued, were sufficiently severe to suggest that in many instances—considerably more than we would expect—our belief that someone deserves certain treatment because of something good or bad that she has done is unjustified. In Chapter Two I followed this up with an examination of the more familiar argument against desert based on determinism, and concluded that this argument was sound. In the third chapter I used the preceding arguments, together with some other considerations, to undermine the retributivist theory of punishment, according to which desert is the key to justifiable punishment. In the next two chapters I developed a utilitarian alternative to retributive punishment and, in the following two, I explained the implications of my views for distributive justice and for the practice of blaming wrongdoers for their bad actions.

If my arguments are accepted, then I may be considered to have shown that appeals to desert based on moral actions or qualities, or on effort-making, have no legitimate place within moral thinking. But even if this is accepted at a theoretical level, there is a clear practical problem. Outside the realms of psychiatry and popular psychology, which may be considered mostly anti-blame (or at least anti-guilt), our societies are very pro-blame and pro-desert, favoring especially, it seems, appeals to negative desert. In fact the latter appears to have the very centrality and importance within the popular understanding of morality as I wish to deny it within a considered and reflective system of ethics. Most people take it for granted that wrongdoers deserve blame and, in more serious cases, punishment. The media in all societies that I know of bolster this attitude, and so do governments. Both usually appear unaware of any method of tackling a social problem other than by identifying supposedly culpable individuals or groups and punishing them. The nightly news bulletins gravely intone the latest plan to 'crack down' on some wrongdoing or other. To 'solve' a problem is to make someone suffer for it. Of course, we know from our previous reflections that punishment can be an effective way of preventing wrongdoing. But this fact does not justify a knee-jerk recourse to punitive action in every case. However, precisely because this attitude is a reflection of a cast of mind deeply entrenched within our societies, people are often slow to recognize the benefits of a different approach. To take one example, it has only recently been realized that the best way of tackling the problem of medical error may not be to punish the doctors concerned, for this makes them prone to engage in cover-ups, which in turn makes it difficult to obtain the information needed to avoid such errors in the future.

In my view the unthinking preference for punitive methods is to a large extent motivated by a desire for vengeance, whether self-acknowledged or not. People seeking punishment for its own sake often claim that it is justice, rather than vengeance, that they seek. But apart from a commitment to certain rules of procedure (which is admittedly welcome), it is hard to see the difference.[1]

What can consequentialists who reject the prevalent obsession with desert and vengeance do in this situation? They could try philosophical argument of the sort offered in this book, but their audience will inevitably be limited. Somewhat more widespread understanding might be achieved through popularizing scientific arguments from psychology which show how people are, in various ways, determined by their circumstances. But while the audience for popular science may be slightly larger than for philosophy, it is still relatively small. Another method—one with potentially larger reach—is the effective use of social or political rhetoric. There is nothing wrong with this, as long as it is kept distinct from the rational activity which generates the underlying ideas. For example, having established through rational means that determinism is probably both true and incompatible with desert, one is entitled to use more emotional means to persuade people not to judge harshly those who cannot help their badness. A useful technique here is to ask the audience whether they themselves are sure that they would have behaved any differently if they had been subject to the same influences as the wrongdoer. Of course, it takes a certain sensitivity to be receptive even to techniques such as this, and there will be many left unmoved by them.

An old adage has it that 'to understand all is to forgive all,' and in essence, that has been the main message of this book. Since trying to understand is a rational obligation, the conclusion should be evident, despite the fact that many resist it so adamantly.

Notes

1. Of course, *distributive* justice (the subject of Chapter 6) is not the same as vengeance, but it is not distributive justice that these people have in mind.

APPENDIX
FORMAL STATEMENT OF THE S-SCORE ALGORITHM

The formal statement of the S-score algorithm which appears below is provided for the purposes of rigor and precision. It is not envisioned that those who would actually be using the algorithm would learn it in this form. A more informal presentation such as that given in Chapter Five, together with plenty of examples, would be needed for that purpose.

I assume an ontology of individual persons and actions (represented by upper case letters) together with descriptions of individual persons and actions (represented by lower case letters). The descriptions correspond to the 'offence types' referred to in Chapter Five.

An *object pair* is an ordered pair $<X, A>$ such that X is an action and A is a person. A *description pair* is an ordered pair $<x, a>$ such that x is a description of a possible action and a is a description of a possible person. An object pair $<X, A>$ is said to *answer to* a description pair $<x, a>$, if and only if X answers to x and A answers to a.

A description pair $<x', a'>$ is a *strengthening* of $<x, a>$, if and only if it satisfies one of the following:

(i) x' is a strengthening of x and a' is logically equivalent to a OR
(ii) x' is logically equivalent to x and a' is a strengthening of a OR
(iii) x' is a strengthening of x and a' is a strengthening of a.

We now list a series of *C-conditions* concerning a description pair $<y, b>$.

(CC1)   Actions answering to y performed by agents answering to b are *mala prohibita*.

(CC2)   Actions answering to y performed by agents answering to b are *mala prohibita and* are likely or certain to result in only short-term harm (i.e. significant but temporary distress or pain) for one or more individuals.

(CC3) Actions answering to *y* performed by agents answering to *b* are likely, but not certain, to create long-term, non-disastrous harm for a limited number of individuals.

(CC4) Actions answering to *y* performed by agents answering to *b* are likely, but not certain, to create long-term non-disastrous harm for a large number of individuals.

(CC5) Actions answering to *y* performed by agents answering to *b* are likely, but not certain, to create disastrous harm for a limited number of individuals.

(CC6) Actions answering to *y* performed by agents answering to *b* are likely, but not certain, to create disastrous harm for a large number of individuals.

(CC7) Actions answering to *y* performed by agents answering to *b* are certain to create long-term non-disastrous harm for a limited number of individuals.

(CC8) Actions answering to *y* performed by agents answering to *b* are certain to create long-term non-disastrous harm for a large number of individuals.

(CC9) Actions answering to *y* performed by agents answering to *b* are certain to create disastrous harm for a limited number of individuals.

(CC10) Actions answering to *y* performed by agents answering to *b* are certain to create disastrous harm for a large number of individuals.

(CC11) Actions answering to *y* performed by agents answering to *b* are performed by more than one individual in combination and the agent answering to *b* is an accomplice rather than a ringleader.

A description pair <*x, a*> is said to *satisfy* a C-condition if and only if the result of substituting '*x*' for '*y*' and '*a*' for '*b*' in the C-condition would yield a truth.

Formal Statement of the S-score Algorithm

We now stipulate that an object pair $<X, A>$ is *criminal* with respect to a set α of C-conditions containing at least one of (CC1) – (CC10), if and only if:

For some description pair $<x, a>$ to which $<X, A>$ answers:

(i) α is the set of all C-conditions C such that it is generally known by people answering to a that $<x, a>$ satisfies C;[1]

(ii) We know of no strengthening $<x', a'>$ of $<x, a>$ to which $<X, A>$ answers such that there is a (possibly empty) set β such that:

   (a) β is the set of all C-conditions C such that it is generally known by people answering to a' that $<x',a'>$ satisfies C;

   (b) β is not identical to α.

I hope that the foregoing is mostly self-explanatory, given a grasp of the material in Section 5.2, though I perhaps should explain clause (ii) of the last definition. This is needed because of the possibility (discussed with slightly different terminology under 'Specificity of action types' at the end of Section 5.2) that there may be, for a given description pair satisfying one or more of the C-clauses, a more specific description pair that satisfies a different set of C-clauses, in which case the latter 'trumps' the former (provided the knowledge condition explained here and in Section 5.2 is satisfied with respect to it). By requiring that $<x, a>$ satisfy (ii), we ensure that it is not considered criminal with respect to the relevant set of C-conditions unless we know of *no* strengthening of $<x, a>$ that would correspond to a 'trumping' offence-type of this kind.

We now define the C-score of $<X, A>$ with respect to α, $C(X,A,\alpha)$, using the following set of rules:

(i) If $<X, A>$ is not criminal with respect to α, $C(X,A,\alpha) = 0$;

(ii) If $<X, A>$ is criminal with respect to α, $C(X,A,\alpha)$ is determined by the following procedure:[2]

   (a) Set $C(X,A,\alpha)$ to zero initially;
   (b) If (CC1) $\in \alpha$, then set $C(X,A,\alpha)$ to 1.
   (c) If (CC2) $\in \alpha$, then set $C(X,A,\alpha)$ to 2.
   (d) If any of (CC3) - (CC10) are in α, set $C(X,A,\alpha)$ to the *serious harm value for α* (defined below).
   (e) If (CC11) $\in \alpha$, then halve the value of $C(X,A,\alpha)$.

Definition of the serious harm value for α:

(i) For each C-condition $C \in \alpha$ from amongst (CC3)-(CC10):

   (a) determine the values of h, n and p as follows:

   for long-term, non-disastrous harm $h = 4$;
   for disastrous harm $h = 8$;

   for a limited number of people $n = 1$;
   for a large number of people $n = 2$;

   for mere likelihood $p = 1$;
   for certainty or near-certainty $p = 2$;

   (b) find the product hnp.

(ii) The serious harm value for α is the highest such product for all the C-conditions $C \in \alpha$ from amongst (CC3)-(CC10).

Finally, let $X_1, X_2, \ldots X_n$ be all the distinct actions[3] of an agent A being considered in a given sentencing episode such that, for each X_i, $<X_i, A>$ is criminal with respect to some α_i. Then the S-score for A in this sentencing episode is:

$\Sigma \, C(X_i, A, \alpha_i)$ for $i = 1$ to n.

NOTES

1. Admittedly, we have to understand this, and similar statements, in a slightly loose way. For example, in the sense of 'knows' relevant here, to know that the lion is a member of the set of mammals, it is sufficient to know that the lion is a mammal. No explicit knowledge of set theory is required. The same goes for metalinguistic knowledge when we talk of 'satisfying' and so on. This is to be understood in terms of knowing the corresponding first-order facts.

2. The clauses are to be worked through in order like a typical computer algorithm, so that the final value of $C(X, A, \alpha)$ is the value assigned to it by the last applicable clause.

3. I intend a straightforward intuitive understanding of this phrase so that, for example, two entirely distinct thefts occurring at different times are two different actions, whereas, if someone steals a suitcase, there are not two distinct

ferent actions, whereas, if someone steals a suitcase, there are not two distinct actions, one of stealing something and another of stealing a suitcase. I am not saying that the latter conception is absolutely mistaken, just that it is not the one I need here. (I handle such distinctions differently, by recognising a multiplicity of action *types*, which a single action may instantiate.)

REFERENCES

Andenaes, Johs. 1971. 'General Prevention—Illusion or Reality?' in Grupp 1971.
Arthur, John and Shaw, William H. (ed.). 1978. *Justice and Economic Distribution*. Englewood Cliffs, N.J.: Prentice-Hall.
Ayer, A.J. 1946. *Language, Truth and Logic*. London: Victor Gollancz (second edition).
Bentham, Jeremy. 1988. *The Principles of Morals and Legislation*. Amherst, NY: Prometheus Books.
Blackburn, Simon. 1984. *Spreading the Word*. Oxford: Oxford University Press.
Blackstone, William. 2008. *An Abridgment Of Blackstone's Commentaries On The Laws Of England (1853)*. Whitefish, Montana: Kessinger.
Cohen, Gerald. 1992. 'Incentives, Inequality and Community' in Petersen 1992, 263-329.
Corlett, J. Angelo. 2004. 'Evil', *Analysis*, 64(1): 81-4.
———2006. *Responsibility and Punishment*. Dordrecht, The Netherlands: Springer (3rd edition).
Dennett, Daniel. 1978. *Brainstorms*. Montgomery, Vermont: Bradford Books.
Duff, R.A. 2001. *Punishment, Communication and Community*. Oxford: Oxford University Press.
Ewing, A.C. 1929. *The Morality of Punishment*. London: Kegan Paul, Trench, Trubner.
Ezorsky, Gertrude (ed.). 1972a. *Philosophical Perspectives on Punishment*. New York: State University of New York Press.
———1972b. 'The Ethics of Punishment' in Ezorsky 1972a, xxiv-xxvii.
Feinberg, Joel. 1970. *Doing and Deserving*. Princeton N.J.: Princeton University Press.
Feldman, Fred. 1997. *Utilitarianism, Hedonism and Desert: essays in moral philosophy*. Cambridge: Cambridge University Press.
Fischer, John Martin. 1994. *The Metaphysics of Free Will: an Essay on Control*. Cambridge, Massachusetts: Blackwell.
Foot, Philippa (ed.). 1967. *Theories of Ethics*. Oxford: Oxford University Press.
Frankfurt, Harry G. 1969. 'Alternate Possibilities and Moral Responsibility,' *Journal of Philosophy*, 66(23), 829-839.

French, Peter. 2001. *The Virtues of Vengeance*. Lawrence, Kansas: University Press of Kansas.
Ginet, Carl. 1966. 'Might We Have No Choice?' in Lehrer 1966.
Glover, Jonathan. 1977. *Causing Death and Saving Lives*. Reading: Penguin Books.
Golash, Deirdre. 1994. 'The Retributive Paradox,' *Analysis*, 54(2): 72-8.
Grupp, Stanley E. (ed.). 1971. *Theories of Punishment*. Bloomington: Indiana University Press.
Haji, Ishtiyaque. 2002. Review of first edition of Corlett 2006, *Mind*, 111(444): 847-851.
Hart, H.L.A. 1963. *Punishment and Responsibility: Essays in the Philosophy of Law*. Oxford: Oxford University Press.
Hegel, G.W.F. 1942. *The Philosophy of Right* (translated by T. Knox). Oxford: Oxford University Press.
Honderich, Ted. 2002. *How free are you? The Determinism Problem*. Oxford: Oxford University Press.
——— 2006. *Punishment: The Supposed Justifications Revisited*. London and Ann Arbor MI: Pluto Press.
Hume, David. 1955. *An Inquiry Concerning Human Understanding*. Indianapolis, New York: The Bobbs-Merrill Company.
James, William. 1890. *The Principles of Psychology vol. 2*. London: MacMillan.
La Follette, Hugh. 1978. 'Why Libertarianism is Mistaken' in Arthur and Shaw 1978, 194-206.
Lehrer, Keith (ed.). 1966. *Freedom and Determinism*. New York: Random House.
Locke, John. 1693. *Some Thoughts Concerning Education*. www.bartleby.com.
Mackie, J.L. 1985. *Persons and Values: selected papers vol. 2*. Oxford: Oxford University Press.
Mill, John Stuart. 1910. *Utilitarianism, On Liberty and Considerations on Representative Government*. London: J.M. Dent and sons.
Moore, G.E. 1993. *Principia Ethica*. Cambridge: Cambridge University Press (revised edition).
Morris, Herbert. 1968. 'Persons and Punishment,' *The Monist*, 52: 475-501.
Murphy, Jeffrie G. and Hampton, Jean. 1988. *Forgiveness and Mercy*. Cambridge: Cambridge University Press.
Nagel, Thomas. 1979. *Mortal Questions*. Cambridge: Cambridge University Press.
Otsuka, Michael. 1998. 'Incompatibilism and the Avoidance of Blame,' *Ethics*, 108(4), 685-701.
Nozick, Robert. 1981. *Philosophical Explanations*. Oxford: Oxford University Press.
——— 2001. *Anarchy, State and Utopia*. Oxford: Blackwell.
Pereboom, Derk. 2001. *Living Without Free Will*. Cambridge: Cambridge University Press.

Petersen, Grethe (ed.). 1992. *The Tanner Lectures on Human Values, vol. 13*. Salt Lake City: University of Utah Press.

Pojman, Louis P. and Reiman, Jeffrey. 1998. *The Death Penalty: For and Against*. Lanham: Rowman and Littlefield.

Quinton, A. 1954. 'On Punishment,' *Analysis*: 133-142.

Rawls, John. 1955. 'Two Concepts of Rules,' *Philosophical Review*, 64(1): 3-32, reprinted in Foot 1967, 144-170.

——1999. *A Theory of Justice*. Cambridge, Mass: Harvard University Press (revised edition).

Reiman, Jeffrey. 1998. 'Why the Death Penalty should be abolished in America', in Pojman and Reiman 1998.

Rescher, Nicholas. 1993. *Moral Luck* in Statman 1993, 154-5.

Richards, Norvin. 1993. *Luck and Desert* in Statman 1993, 175-7.

Ryle, Gilbert. 1949. *The Concept of Mind*. Harmondsworth, Middlesex: Penguin Books.

Sher, George. 1987. *Desert*. Princeton: Princeton University Press.

——2006. *In Praise of Blame*. Oxford: Oxford University Press.

Singer, Peter. 1978. 'Rights and the Market' in Arthur and Shaw 1978, 207-221.

Slote, Michael. 1995. 'Agent-based Virtue Ethics,' *Midwest Studies in Philosophy*, 20.

Smart, J.J.C. and Williams, Bernard. 1973. *Utilitarianism: for and against*. Cambridge: Cambridge University Press.

Smith, Holly. 1983. 'Culpable Ignorance,' The Philosophical Review, 92(4): 543-571.

Statman, Daniel (ed.). 1993. *Moral Luck*. Albany: State University of New York Press.

Strawson, P.F. 1974. *Freedom and Resentment and other essays*. London: Methuen, 1974.

Thomson, Judith Jarvis. 1993. *Morality and Bad Luck* in Statman 1993.

Waller, Bruce. 1999. 'Deep Thinkers, Cognitive Misers and Moral Responsibility,' *Analysis*, 59(4): 223-9.

Zaibert, Leo. 2005. *Five Ways Patricia Can Kill her Husband*. Chicago and La Salle, Illinois: Open Court Publishing Company.

Zimmerman, Michael J. 1988. *An Essay on Moral Responsibility*. Totowa, New Jersey: Rowman and Littlefield.

——1993. 'Luck and Moral Responsibility' in Statman 1993, 226-9.

INDEX

A

Andenaes, Johs, 72
Ayer, A.J., 16, 91

B

Bentham, Jeremy, 87–89, 117, 118
Blackburn, Simon, 16
Blackstone, William, 47
blame, 3, 15, 16, 19, 21, 23, 26, 29, 31, 41, 48, 58, 81, 124, 132, 133, 134, 135–39, 140, 141
  and determinism, 27–28
  and internalism, 4–8

C

character, 5, 9, 8–10, 14, 16, 67, 69, 70, 91, 115, 121, 135, 136, 138, 139
Christianity, 92, 132
Clockwork Orange, 85
Cohen, Gerald, 126
compatibilism, 19–24
Corlett, J. Angelo, 35, 39, 45–58, 128
C-score, 92–105, 106, 107, 111, 145

D

death penalty, 47, 52, 53, 71, 90
Dennett, Daniel, 30
desert, 65, 3, 4, 15, 16, 17, 20, 22, 24, 26, 61, 66, 71, 77, 89, 97, 101, 106, 109, 112, 113, 125, 127, 129, 132, 136, 137, 141, 142
  and character, 8–10
  and effort, 121–25
  and knowledge, 7
  and mental difficulty, 7–8
  and superfluous suffering, 10–13
  as basis of punishment, 33–60
  defined, 35
  internalist view, 4–8
  positive, 13–15, 121–28
  within utilitarianism, 80–83

determinism, 19–30, 44, 54, 57, 58, 60, 73, 75, 77, 81, 82, 83
  biological vs. psychological, 24–26
  hard vs. soft, 19–20
diachronic fairness, 12
Difference Principle (Rawls), 126–27
Duff, R.A., 61, 69–70, 75–77, 79, 80, 84, 85, 110

E

egalitarianism, 38, 127, 128
equality, 38, 37–38, 120, 125, 126, 127, 128
Ewing, A.C., 72
exculpation, 101, 105–13
expected harm, 3
externalism, 4, 5, 7
Ezorsky, Gertrude, 16

F

Feinberg, Joel, 17, 84
Feldman, Fred, 4
Fischer, John Martin, 30, 44, 58
foreknowledge, 30
forgiveness, 48, 54–55, 132
Frankfurt cases, 22–24
Frankfurt, Harry, 22, 31
free will, 19–30, 74, 83
French, Peter, 5, 39–44, 45, 57, 58, 62, 132, 133

G

Ginet, Carl, 30
Glover, Jonathan, 71
Golash, Deirdre, 62
guilt, 29, 41, 69, 80, 81, 134, 137, 141

H

Haji, Ishtiyaque, 63
Hampton, Jean, 37–39, 62

Hart, Gary, 9, 19, 52, 95, 101–2, 103
Hart, H.L.A., 34
Hegel, G.W.F., 75
Hitler, Adolf, 58, 59
Honderich, Ted, 22, 25, 30, 31, 61, 62, 83, 84
Humanity, Principle of (Honderich), 127
Hume, David, 30

I

incompatibilism, 20, 22, 23, 28, 30, 44
internalism, 4–8, 14

J

James, William, 124, 128
justice, 4, 40, 47, 50, 51, 68, 81, 82, 142
   criminal, 47, 55, 77, 78, 80, 90, 100, 105, 113, 119, 134
   distributive, 82, 85, 121, 122, 125–28, 132, 141, 142

L

La Follette, Hugh, 125
libertarianism, 19, 24–26, 30
Locke, John, 120, 125

M

Mackie, J.L., 36, 61
mens rea, 2–4, 8, 33, 39, 41, 61, 81
mercy, 48, 54–55
Mill, John Stuart, 118
Moore, G.E., 36, 61
moral appraisal, 4, 11, 28, 121, 141
Morris, Herbert, 60
motivation, 14, 21, 26, 42, 67, 121
murder, 5–6, 39, 48, 52, 87, 90, 91, 95, 103, 106, 108, 109, 113
Murphy, Jeffrie, 52, 63

N

Nagel, Thomas, 9, 31

negligence, 2, 3–4, 62, 97
Nozick, Robert, 31, 40, 62, 125

O

Otsuka, Michael, 23, 31

P

Pereboom, Derk, 28
praise, 13–15, 18, 21, 26, 27, 58, 121, 132, 135
punishment, 13, 14, 15, 18, 20, 22, 23, 30, 31, 33–117, 121, 125, 128, 132, 134, 141, 142
   as deterrence, 67, 71–72, 87–88, 91–113
   as incapacitation, 67, 70–71, 90–91
   as reform, 67
   as reparation, 67–68
   as retribution, 33–60
   'educative' function, 67, 72
   of children, 114–17

Q

quantum theory, 20
Quinton, Anthony, 61

R

Rawls, John, 80, 82, 85, 122, 123, 124, 125–27
recklessness, 2–3, 4, 9, 52, 62
Reiman, Jeffrey, 46
reparation, 51, 54, 55, 56, 67, 68
Rescher, Nicholas, 16
restitution. *See* reparation
retributive balance, 10, 12, 13, 15, 17, 57, 82
retributivism, 16, 22, 31, 33–60, 61, 62, 66, 69
revenge. *See* vengeance
reward, 13–15, 58, 74, 75, 82, 115, 121, 122, 123, 127, 135
Richards, Norvin, 16
Ryle, Gilbert, 128

S

Selby Rail Disaster, 65, 52
self, 5, 24–26, 31
Sher, George, 12, 15, 37, 81, 82, 85, 122–25, 139
Singer, Peter, 125
Slote, Michael, 42
Smart, J.J.C., 83
Smith, Holly, 15
Sorell, Tom, 16
S-score, 92–105, 107, 108, 117, 143–46
state-assisted suicide, 91, 117
Strawson, P.F., 61, 139
supererogatory acts, 13, 14, 48

T

temptation, 8, 13, 14, 81, 88, 89, 113, 117, 132, 135
Thomson, Judith Jarvis, 4

U

utilitarianism, 33, 34, 43, 44, 46, 50, 51, 54, 60, 61, 63, 66–117, 118, 127, 128, 133, 135, 141

V

vengeance, 5, 39-44, 45, 142
victims, 5, 46, 53, 68, 69, 70, 71, 77, 103
virtual killer, 5–6, 14
volition, 124
voluntary acts, 22, 124, 125

W

Wallenberg, Raoul, 59, 60
Waller, Bruce, 22
weak reasons-responsiveness, 30, 44
Williams, Bernard, 83

Z

Zaibert, Leo, 16
Zimmerman, Michael, 6, 16, 135

www.ingramcontent.com/pod-product-compliance
Lightning Source LLC
Chambersburg PA
CBHW021832300426
44114CB00009BA/413